TO WEEP FOR A STRANGER:

COMPASSION FATIGUE IN CAREGIVING

By Patricia Smith

TO WEEP FOR A STRANGER:

COMPASSION FATIGUE IN CAREGIVING

By Patricia Smith

Founder, Compassion Fatigue Awareness Project©

✺

Dedicated with love to my lifelong caregivers:

My Mom,

Gloria Carmichael

&

My Sisters,

Terry O'Donnell & Ann Deggelman

✺

✳

Acknowledgements

To Blake, Derek and Elizabeth Smith, my three children, whose support for my compassion fatigue work has been endless. The thoughts and ideas you have shared continue to shape everything I do. To Laura Lutz. I don't know where to start. Your comments and edits helped considerably. Thank you for taking the time to read through the manuscript. To Shona Robertson and Carin Jacobs, my two brilliant friends, who have spent hours and hours on the phone with me defining and identifying feelings and insights into tangible ideas and words. To Dr. Charles Figley and Dr. Beth Hudnall-Stamm, two wonderful teachers, who generously share their knowledge and materials with us neophytes. And lastly, to all of the kind and loving caregivers who have contacted me and shared their personal and professional tales via the Compassion Fatigue Awareness Project©. You are making the world a better place one story at a time.

✳

Table of Contents

Introduction..11

Chapter One: When Caring Too Much Hurts............................17

Chapter Two: What is Compassion Fatigue?...........................27

Chapter Three: Burdens of the Chosen..................................45

Chapter Four: The Decision to Heal......................................67

Chapter Five: Standards of Self-Care....................................87

Chapter Six: To Family Caregivers.......................................99

Chapter Seven: To Those Entering the Helping Professions..105

Chapter Eight: When the Workplace Suffers..........................119

Chapter Nine: To Weep for a Stranger..................................125

✳

"As a shepherd once so rightly said,
although heaven knows where he learned it,
one can show no greater respect
than to weep for a stranger."
    - Jose Saramago

✳

Introduction

Many years ago, my oldest son recommended that I become familiar with the works of Joseph Campbell. First published in 1949, Campbell's book, *The Hero with a Thousand Faces,* describes the stages of a journey taken when one is summoned by "a calling." I was completely taken with this foray into mythology. To think that an ordinary person living in an ordinary world could be called to venture out of his circle of comfort and thrust into the world of the unknown was exhilarating!

According to Campbell, the "hero" first hears a call to adventure. If he agrees to travel the path, the road of trials lies ahead. Ultimately, the hero must survive a severe challenge either alone or with assistance. If he survives this grueling test, in return he receives a gift – also known as the goal or the boon. If the hero decides to return to his ordinary world, he carries with him great powers and the gift of self-knowledge. He then manifests his new-found strength into action and improves the world. This step in the process is known as the application of the boon.

When reading Campbell's book many years ago, I had no idea that I was reading my future. His words formed the foundation of what I was to experience in my own life. My Hero's Journey was not fraught with prehistoric monsters, jungle-laden terrains or death-defying stunts. Although there were times when I felt frightfully alone. My "calling" wasn't a loud, booming voice from above urging me to take a chance. It actually felt more like a nudge. There were times when discouragement felt like intense failure and times when success felt like I had scaled a mountain and reached the pinnacle. But most of the time, it was just plain old hard work.

The nudge occurred in a very ordinary setting - in my cubicle where I worked as a training and development manager for my local animal shelter. My boss approached me to create a shelter-wide training on compassion fatigue. I had never heard the phrase before, but I was certainly willing to venture out and do some research. One of the first materials I located was Dr. Beth Hudnall-Stamm's Professional Quality of Life Self-Test, which rated levels of compassion satisfaction, burnout, and vicarious trauma (VT). After taking the test, I discovered that my scores were sky-high, sparking a journey of self-discovery that continues today. My Hero's Journey hurled me through the maze of unhealthy habits to applying authentic, sustainable self-care practices that allow me to create good health in my life.

It didn't take long to realize that my knowledge and understanding of compassion fatigue and how to manage the symptoms could be helpful to others. I put together a workshop and before I knew it, I was presenting several workshops a month. I branched out and presented for groups of social workers, hospice personnel, medical practitioners and child advocates. The situations varied, but the symptoms were the same. It was then that I began to realize the scope of compassion fatigue within the helping professions. When a national organization that advocates rights for both animals and children asked me to come onboard as a consultant, I jumped at the chance.

After presenting workshops nation-wide for over a year, meeting people from every corner of the country, I began to comprehend how deeply the underlying mechanisms of compassion fatigue take hold of a caregiver's life. In my travels, I met myriad caregivers from all professions. Each one had a story to tell, and I listened. I soon realized that at the core, every story was the same, only the details differed. Every story told of legacies of disenfranchisement, oppression, invalidation. The pain and suffering compassion fatigue was causing varied from mild to extensive. I had no choice but to share my experience and the body of knowledge I had gathered during the course of my own journey. I had conquered the trials and tribulations to create a life filled with happiness, peace and well-being. My "boon" was to share my experiences with others.

I created the Compassion Fatigue Awareness Project© as a vehicle to bring others into the circle of authentic, sustainable self-care. Since it isn't possible for me to accept every speaking/ workshop engagement, I've created *Healthy Caregiving: A Guide to Recognizing and Managing Compassion Fatigue*. There is both a presenter's guide and a student guide. Hopefully, these workbooks are a step in the right direction which allow those who are asked to present a workshop can become proficient at training in order to share with others.

The book you are about to read is somewhat of an introduction to compassion fatigue. The basics are here – the definition of compassion fatigue, its symptoms and causes, and some standards of self-care that will set you on the path to well-being. I've also included chapters on organizational compassion fatigue, family caregivers and a special chapter to those who are just starting out in the helping professions. An awareness of compassion fatigue before setting out in a caregiving profession could save you years of pain and suffering. Compassion fatigue can be avoided with the right information.

It is no coincidence that you have opened this book. David Carr, Professor of Library Science at the University of North Carolina at Chapel Hill and an expert on learning tells us:

> *"Most of our learning is less accidental than we may think. We really have to want it to happen. The accident that teaches us is one we have been prepared to have, the one we had hoped in the dark for. No learning happens*

to us that we do not somehow need or want to happen to us. And we can marshal powerful personal forces of resistance when we wish to avoid a lesson. Yet we can work....to make our learning fit....our vision of our future selves, the selves we wish most to become."

We all have an opportunity to embark on our own Hero's Journey. Possibly, reading this book will set you on a course of self-discovery that could change your life for the better. I certainly hope so. If you are already in the process, don't lose hope! New patterns and behaviors take time. Chances are that you've never acquired the necessary coping skills to create a life that fulfills your needs, dreams and desires. You are now beginning an important phase of your life and if you agree to the journey and learn the lessons it presents, your hard work will reap benefits you never thought possible.

Patricia Smith
Mountain View, California
May, 2009

❋

✺

CHAPTER ONE: WHEN CARING TOO MUCH HURTS

Several years ago, I hosted a bridal shower for a niece. I noticed my friend Nancy was unduly quiet. Since I was one of the organizers and busy with guests, several hours passed before I was able to approach her. Finally, we met up in the kitchen.

"Nancy," I said. "Are you okay? You seem unusually quiet."

"I'm not doing well at all," she replied. "I realize that I've given so much throughout my life and have gotten very little in return."

Needless to say, I was stunned. Her frankness was completely uncharacteristic. In my recollection, Nancy – wife, mother of four, grandmother and great-grandmother to many – had never expressed such intensely personal feelings in the 40-plus years I'd known her. Throughout the years, she had quietly raised her family, oversaw their household, and in later years, worked as a nursing attendant in the oncology ward at a nearby hospital. By the look of weariness on her face, it seemed everything had come crashing down and she was most likely in crisis. Since I had been facilitating compassion fatigue workshops for over a year, I was able to easily recognize the classic symptoms.

"Have you ever heard the term 'compassion fatigue?'" I asked. Her tired eyes brightened and her slumped body lifted slightly. I could see the words ignited a hint of hope in her depressed emotions. Perhaps *someone* understood what she was going through.

"I'm recovering from compassion fatigue," she answered in a matter-of-fact monotone.

Every day, caregivers from diverse sectors such as animal welfare, medical and social services are realizing what it has taken Nancy many years to acknowledge: Caring too much can hurt. Many caregivers are not aware that the stress they are experiencing in their lives actually has a name: compassion fatigue. When caregivers focus on others without sustaining healthy self-care practices, a wide range of destructive behaviors can surface.

Due to a lack of understanding about this cycle, sufferers often view themselves in negative ways, applying such labels as burnout, over-reactive, unprofessional or possessing a savior complex. A delightful, intelligent man in one of my workshops sadly referred to himself as "unrelentlessly average." Unfortunately, others often jump in and apply additional labels compounding the situation further. Left unattended, compassion fatigue can extol a very high price on all aspects of a caregiver's life.

So, what is this thing called compassion fatigue? The actual definition is this: compassion fatigue is a secondary traumatic stress syndrome. The symptoms are a natural consequence of stress resulting from caring for and helping traumatized or suffering people or animals. It is a set of symptoms, not a disease. The outward signs that actualize compassion fatigue in our lives are displays of stress resulting from giving care to others. As responders to those in pain or those who are suffering, we leave ourselves open to incorporating their trauma as our own. The label compassion fatigue has been attached to the symptoms so that it is identifiable in caregivers. Unfortunately, those of us most at-risk for compassion fatigue use a common method of coping with the discomfort we experience, and that is to stifle the uncomfortable feelings and emotions. Sometimes it is the only way we can continue to do our caregiving work.

Caregivers come in all colors, sizes, shapes and degrees of education. Some are young students, eager to make a mark on the caregiving profession of choice. Others hail from trade schools, such as LVNs or animal welfare technicians, who want to do their share in making the world a better place. Others are highly-trained professionals such as doctors, nurses, attorneys, mediators and social workers. And, sadly, others are thrust into the helping profession as family caregivers when a loved one is stricken with a serious or terminal illness. No matter what the origin of your caregiving profession, it is now common knowledge that compassion fatigue is plaguing thousands, if not millions, of caregivers worldwide, subjecting them to a life mired in personal pain and suffering, as well as disillusionment about their caregiving choices.

All of this leads us to the question at the heart of the matter: Why caregiving? Why do certain people feel a draw, a pull, and often a "calling" to go into a caregiving profession? Some even explain the experience as "being chosen." In order to understand more about this phenomenon, it is best to start where most of our thoughts, ideas and patterns begin – childhood.

Consider these three statements:

- When asked how it is possible to expend such enormous efforts caring for terminally ill babies who will die despite all efforts, Mother Teresa replied that the sheer act of love transcends its outcome.

- Those whom God wishes to bless, goes the saying, He puts in their hands the means of helping others.

- Give 'til it hurts.

Pronouncements such as the three above reflect the world's love affair with those who care for others. Noble, loving, unselfish and good are, arguably, words that most people would bestow on those who choose to work or volunteer in the helping professions. To be cared for and valued are basic human needs that most people admit to having. And those who dare to fill those needs in others are revered and held in high esteem. With such warm and fuzzy quotes and kudos, it's a wonder everyone doesn't aspire to enter a caregiving profession!

But the truth of the matter is, they don't. Reasons, such as inadequate pay or a dislike of working with sick people, are often enough motivation for students to pass over human service courses and fill up on business or technology units. These reasons do hold water. Historically, salaries in the caregiving professions are low, and caring for the sick, aged and infirm is by no means a glamour job. As for women returning to the workplace, our capitalistic society simply doesn't value the skills and talents they have developed in the caring and feeding of their families.

So, what does this say about those of us who feel the strong, magnetic pull of providing care to others? What is it that causes us to gravitate toward jobs that others won't even consider? Or more emphatically, refuse to do?

Many have attempted to answer these thought-provoking questions. In 2001, *Conscious Choice* writer Michael Hansen penned a column entitled: *Battling Compassion Fatigue: The Pitfalls and Promise of Modern Altruism*. Reading his ideas regarding the causes of compassion fatigue might lead us to believe that maybe we are genetically predisposed to caregiving. He writes:

> *"Selfless behavior toward the community is also easily explainable. It's become increasingly obvious that the human species spent the majority of its existence as*

pack predators- as animals to whom submersion in the consensual goals and priorities of the tribe were vital to species survival. Concepts like heroism, charity or community were not abstracts or ideals – they were the day-to-day necessities for the continuing survival of the pack, the tribe."

Continuing on, he suggests that, perhaps, caregivers are motivated by sheer love.

"Undoubtedly, love was sufficient reason to those early caregivers. More than one archeological dig has revealed the remains of people with disabling injuries, who apparently lived for long periods of time after being crippled – someone had to have fed them."

While his arguments support the idea that our ancestors were caregivers out of necessity in order to survive, he readily admits that it's a stretch to apply their motives to members of our modern day society. While we, as a species, claim to value compassionate care and a respect for all life, in actuality, we don't. Hanson goes on to blame mass media alienation for shutting off society's caregiving valve. He writes:

"Modern civilization is alienating, however: we live among masses of total strangers with workloads and family structures that give us less and less time for community. Our main conduits to society are passive mass media that gives us little chance of human interaction. After a hard day at work, how do you overcome your fatigue enough to make the extension to others around you? How do you reach out and fulfill the needs of a nameless face on the other side of a TV screen? When one needy person after another hits that screen, how do you sidestep compassion fatigue?"

If society is plagued with caregiving obstacles such as alienation, mass media, and everyday fatigue, how do we explain those of us who are still willing to extend ourselves to others? Fulfill the needs of the needy? And tempt compassion fatigue in order to be of service to those who require our care?

Participants in my compassion fatigue workshops have taught me that there are no blanket answers to those questions. Ask twenty different caregivers these questions and you will receive twenty different answers. Whatever the story, these glimpses into what makes caregivers tick are personal, emotional and often, memorable. Responses range from upholding a family tradition to, as one animal welfare worker revealed, paying homage to a dear pet that provided her comfort while growing up in an abusive home.

We each have a special story to tell about how we landed on the caregiving doorstep. Both the big picture and the minute details can vary drastically from person to person, which is what makes this subject both interesting and frustrating at the same time. There are many paths that lead to compassion fatigue. Keep in mind that the purpose of telling our stories, and this is a mandatory element of healing, is not to label each story right or wrong – functional or dysfunctional. We do not share our histories with the intent to criticize or demean our families of origin, our traditions or our cultures. And I certainly don't encourage readers to look back in anger or resentment. In the end, we are who we are and acceptance is the name of the game. The object of telling our stories and then asking some well-placed questions is to promote awareness. If we don't know where we've been, how can we begin to know where we want to go? Author Lewis Carroll said it best when he wrote the following passage in his beloved classic *Alice's Adventures in Wonderland:*

> *One day Alice came to a fork in the road and saw a Cheshire cat in a tree. "Which road do I take?" she asked.*

His response was a question: "Where do you want to go?"
"I don't know," Alice answered. "Then," said the cat, "it
doesn't really matter."

Imagine that you've arrived at your fork in the road in relation to your caregiving. Have you arrived on the scene bursting with clarity about where you are going? Or have you arrived on the scene in a fog with no clue as to why or how you landed there? Or maybe you find yourself somewhere in between? How would you answer the Cheshire cat? Your reply could hold clues as to whether or not you'll encounter compassion fatigue down the road, or perhaps are already a sufferer.

At this point, appropriately, let's go down a quick rabbit hole.

What many of us caregivers don't realize is that our caregiving experiences not only affect our own lives, but the lives of those close to us. Family members, significant others, friends and colleagues are all at-risk due to the traumatic events that we inevitably witness and are compelled to share. When our loved ones support and validate our work by listening to our stories, they, too, absorb the emotional effects second-hand. This is not unlike the process by which we, as caregivers, absorb the emotional effects first-hand of those to whom we give care.

Why does all of this matter? Simply because as you proceed in reading the following pages, it is mandatory that you understand that caregiving, while often misread as a feel-good profession, vocation or avocation is, indeed, very serious emotional work. As you, the reader, begin to comprehend the effects of caregiving on your life thus far, you'll be able to take in the material with an informed mind and heart.

In 2007, the *San Francisco Chronicle* ran an article by Associated Press writer Kevin Freking. He cites the National

Survey on Drug Use and Health, a U.S. government survey and reported the following:

> "*People who tend to the elderly, change diapers and serve up food and drinks have the highest rates of depression among U.S. workers. ...Almost 11 percent of personal care workers – which includes child care and helping the elderly and severely disabled with their daily needs – reported depression lasting two weeks or longer. ...In tie for third were health care workers and social workers at 9.6 percent.*"

This comes as no surprise that caregiving professions can produce depression, burnout and compassion fatigue in workers who are unsuccessful at balancing their self-care regime with caring for others. With the baby boomers aging, we can expect to see an extraordinary amount of caregiving challenges surface.

I first learned about compassion fatigue when working in animal welfare. As the training and development manager at my local animal shelter, I was asked to create a shelter-wide compassion fatigue training. When my boss gave me the assignment, I'd never heard the term. I went online and what I found has changed my life. The more I learned about the secondary traumatic stress syndrome, the more passionate I grew about bringing the information to light. One night while talking to my son Derek on the phone, I happened to mention that if I could do anything it would be to create a place where caregivers could go to learn about compassion fatigue. He asked me, what would you call it? I answered, the Compassion Fatigue Awareness Project. He then said, you just created it. With that, he offered to design a website and the rest is history.

I was fortunate at that point to have access to the work of Dr. Charles Figley, the world's leading traumatologist; Dr. Eric Gentry, with whom I attended compassion fatigue certification training; and Dr. Beth Hudnall-Stamm, who created the ProQOL Self-Test which has been a godsend to those of us learning about this subject. Their years of research and subsequent materials helped to further my knowledge and understanding. But it has been through my website and workshops that I have really come to understand how wide-spread and insidious this secondary traumatic stress syndrome is. I've communicated with people throughout the world who have shared their stories and made it possible for me to continue to learn.

In the coming chapters I hope to guide you through an understanding of how compassion fatigue emerges over the course of helping others. We'll look at the various symptoms that can zap your energy and detract from healthy caregiving. And, finally, how positive outcomes can be experienced, both for you and those to whom you provide care. It is noble to weep for a stranger, but only when we are able to walk beside and not take on his suffering as our own.

If you are a family caregiver reading these pages, please note that I have reserved one full chapter on the challenges you face. Often, we are thrust into the role of caregiver and it is not of our own choosing. Caring for an aging parent, a terminally ill partner, or a chronically ill child can be draining and discouraging. But as with everything difficult in life, there is another side to this challenge; one that can lift the spirits, create hope, and allow us to grow and change for the better.

✳️

✳

CHAPTER TWO: WHAT IS COMPASSION FATIGUE?

There is now a consensus among mental health care professionals that as responders to those in pain and who are suffering, we are capable of absorbing their trauma. When caregivers focus on others without practicing authentic, ongoing self-care, destructive behaviors can surface. Apathy, isolation, bottled up emotions, substance abuse, poor personal hygiene and emotional outbursts head a long list of symptoms associated with the secondary traumatic stress known as compassion fatigue.

Studies confirm that caregivers play host to a high level of compassion fatigue, often without knowledge and awareness of its devastating effect on their lives. Day in, day out, workers struggle to function in caregiving environments that constantly present heart-wrenching, emotional challenges. Affecting positive change in a throw-away society, a mission so vital to those who value being of service to others, is perceived as elusive, if not impossible. This painful reality, coupled with first-hand knowledge of society's flagrant disregard for the safety and well-being of the feeble and frail, takes its toll on everyone from full time employees to part time volunteers. Eventually, negative attitudes can prevail.

When compassion fatigue hits critical mass in the workplace, the organization itself will suffer. Chronic absenteeism, spiraling Worker's Comp claims, high turnover rates, friction between employees, and friction between management and staff are some of the symptoms that surface, creating additional stress on workers. We will take a look at organizational compassion fatigue in *Chapter Eight: When the Workplace Suffers.*

While the effects of compassion fatigue on both the individual and the organization are dismal, chances for recovery and healing are not. That said, there is one dangerous pitfall in acquiring an awareness of compassion fatigue. Once I began to see a marked difference in the quality of my life, I became less diligent in practicing authentic, sustainable self-care. I made some decisions based on my perception of what I could handle as opposed to what I was actually capable of handling. Each time this happened, I found myself back in Square One.

After a year on the road traveling, I decided I needed a home-base and accepted a job as program director for a facility that housed children with life-threatening illnesses. I leaped from the proverbial frying pan into the fire, trading euthanized animals for children with life-threatening illnesses, many of whom died during treatment. Even with all of my knowledge, experience and, dare I say, intelligence, I managed to cascade into yet a deeper level of symptoms. I left that position in worse shape than ever before.

I learned from this particular experience that this program for recognizing and managing compassion fatigue is a lifelong process. The next position I accepted was in a caregiving profession, but I was no longer on the front line or in the trenches continuing to experience the direct trauma of those in pain and who are suffering.

Due to an extraordinary amount of study and research by psychologists in the field of traumatology, we now have the help we need to understand this disorder and a definition. Again, here is the definition:

Compassion fatigue is a secondary traumatic stress

disorder. The display of symptoms is the natural consequence of stress resulting from caring and helping traumatized or suffering people or animals. (Figley,1995).

It is important to reiterate that compassion fatigue is a term, not a disease. The associated symptoms are normal displays of chronic stress resulting from giving care to others. At some time, everyone has experienced one or more of these symptoms simultaneously. The difference between a healthy caregiver and a compassion fatigued caregiver is that with the sufferer, the symptoms are chronic. The headaches never seem to go away; the allergies never seem to clear up. There is a constant need to express the excessive complaints verbally. This is most likely due to very high level of frustration and a lack of awareness as to where the symptoms originated. As an onlooker, you will see the definition of insanity being played out. Insanity is doing the same thing over and over and expecting a different outcome. A set of specific compassion fatigue symptoms include:

- BOTTLED UP EMOTIONS – Outbursts are very common with compassion fatigue sufferers. People who have been taught how to deal with emotions in a healthy manner know how to attend to their feelings, pinpoint the origin, approach the situation in a logical, unemotional way, resolve the issue and move on. Because compassion fatigue has its roots in the psychological makeup of its "victims," it usually strikes those lacking in personal survival skills. The most common unhealthy way of dealing with emotions is to "stuff" them down and then act as if they don't exist. The problem with this method of dealing with personal issues is that humans can, and do, become overstuffed. Once that happens, all control is lost and "blurting" becomes the norm.

- IMPULSE TO RESCUE ANYONE IN NEED - While this symptom runs rampant in the animal welfare world, it can take hold in the life of any caregiver. It isn't uncommon in animal welfare work to have colleagues sharing a living space with 6 dogs, 3 cats, 2 birds, a garter snake and a potbelly pig. The impulse to rescue others, human or otherwise, stems from the need to rescue oneself. Because unhealthy caregivers are "other directed" (we'll discuss this later in the book), they seek answers to life in an outward fashion, as opposed to an inward fashion. Remember that all of the answers we seek are within.

- ISOLATION FROM OTHERS - Ask any compassion fatigued caregiver what s/he does in their spare time and you'll receive the following answer at least 50 percent of the time: I shut the curtains, turn on the television, turn off the phone, grab some fast food and a beer. This sad commentary is due to the fact that by the time they have put in 8-plus hours giving all they've got to others, there is a driving need to put something back. A constant feeling of depletion is present day and night. Drama is always under the surface; life is lived reactively as opposed to pro-actively. Life feels out of control and the need to self-medicate, whether through alcohol, chocolate, tobacco, or drugs seems like the best way to "fill up" and continue on.

- SADNESS, APATHY: When a person is shrouded in a veil of sadness the world is a very gloomy place. Everyone experiences feelings of sadness occasionally, but when the feeling persists and nothing seems to alleviate the depressed emotions, compassion fatigue may be at the heart of the problem. Sadness tied to an apathetic outlook definitely raises a red flag. Sadness and apathy are best recognized in a personality when extreme negativism pervades.

- OFTEN FEELS THE NEED TO VOICE EXCESSIVE

COMPLAINTS ABOUT MANAGEMENT AND CO-WORKERS - At the core of excessive complaining is a feeling of powerlessness. All of the problems are "out there" with management and co-workers. Powerlessness partners with low self-esteem to create a blockade to recognizing problems, raising creative responsible solutions, executing successful outcomes and then moving beyond the frustration and unhealthy attitudes. Unfortunately, many non-profit organizations, where caregiving usually lives, are experiencing multi-level compassion fatigue. The symptoms are present from the top on down. When this happens, the only hope is education and training. Albert Einstein once said: Problems cannot be solved with the same awareness that created them.

- LACK OF INTEREST IN SELF-CARE PRACTICES: At the heart of self-care is self pride. This isn't to say that a person needs to walk around with a haughty attitude. It is about having a pride in oneself. There are many ways to share our self pride with the world, but the most popular is through our appearance. Compassion fatigue can rob us of our feeling of self worth, therefore, we show the world our pain and suffering by letting our hygiene habits dissolve, our exercise program disappear and our sustainable, healthy eating habits fall by the wayside.

- REOCCURRING NIGHTMARES, FLASHBACKS: Perhaps the most disturbing of all symptoms are reoccurring nightmares and flashbacks. We relive the distressing scenes that caused us first-hand trauma. These difficult visions continue to plague our waking and sleeping hours due to the fact that they have not been properly processed and released. The most important thing a compassion fatigue sufferer needs is quality sleep. Unfortunately, the first thing to go when compassion fatigue symptoms surface is restful sleep.

- PERSISTENT PHYSICAL AILMENTS: We all know someone who has allergies, persistent headaches, reoccurring colds or gastrointestinal problems that never seem to end. When internal, psychological pain and suffering are held at bay, deeply within for any length of time, the body will act out that pain and suffering. It does this in the form of persistent ailments that are never healed and the cause is never resolved.

- DIFFICULTIES CONCENTRATING/MENTALLY TIRED: As with the body, the brain continues to decline when sustainable care isn't present. Without sleep, proper nutrition, lack of exercise and a healthy perspective, concentration declines causing overwhelming mental and physical fatigue.

- PRONE TO ACCIDENTS: Without concentration & focus on keeping safe and well, accidents will happen. Plain and simple.

- DEBT/FINANCIAL PROBLEMS: These types of symptoms originate from a lack of taking responsibility for oneself, particularly over a course of time. When the sufferer is other-directed, chances are excellent s/he will not tend to his or her own affairs. This includes such activities as acquiring health insurance, making appointments for annual medical/dental visits, keeping personal items such as automobiles, house or apartment in good repair, and paying bills/registrations/subscriptions in a timely manner. This inability to manage one's own life is borne out of a lack of basic life coping skills and an ability to make good, sound life decisions. Also lacking, basic organizational and time-management skills.

While the term *Compassion Fatigue* entered our vocabulary more than ten years ago, the challenge to caregivers has existed for generations. In his 1933 autobiography *Out of My Life and Thought*, Dr. Albert Schweitzer makes this statement about his medical work in Lambarèné, French Equatorial Africa:

> *Heavy as it was, I found the actual work a lighter burden than the care and responsibility that came with it. Unfortunately, I am among those doctors who do not have the robust temperament desirable for this calling, but who worry about the condition of the seriously ill and of those who have undergone an operation. In vain have I tried to achieve that equanimity that permits the doctor to combine compassion for his patients with the necessary preservation of his own energies.*

In 2002, author Gail Sheehy published an article entitled: *So Much Good Happened Here.* Her words chronicle the aftermath of two terrorist attacks – the bombing of the Alfred P. Murrah Federal Building in Oklahoma City on April 19, 1995 and the attacks on the World Trade Center in New York on September 11, 2001. She wrote:

> *The dismal story of rescue workers in Oklahoma City bombings points to the difficulties now facing PAPD crew and families. Starting 18 months after that terrorist bombing in 1995, police and firefighters began reaping the whirlwind of survivor's guilt – isolation from family and friends, divorces, alcoholism, gambling, and suicides.*

In both cases the words describe what we now recognize as compassion fatigue.

As already mentioned, when a caregiver focuses on others without practicing authentic, on-going self-care practices, destructive behaviors can surface. The symptoms have the ability to disrupt our lives in ways that make everyday living unbearable and produce chronic physical ailments such as headaches, sinus infections, backaches, joint aches, dental problems and eating disorders. When faced with these types of symptoms day in and day out, compassion fatigue sets us up for the domino effect. Maintaining a job when we can barely find our way to the shower in the morning proves difficult at best. Balancing career and relationships present hurdles that overwhelm us. Everyday tasks such as keeping our automobiles maintained or paying bills on time begin to look like Mt. Everest. Simply put, our view of life becomes distorted and, ultimately, unmanageable. This is serious business.

There are people who have the capacity to provide decades of caregiving and never experience any of the symptoms mentioned above. I once worked at a healthcare facility with a nurse I'll call Frederick. As the director of nursing at one of our hospitals, he had high-level responsibilities, managed a 25-member staff, and was a community volunteer as well. What he accomplished in a week would make most people run for the hills. But not Frederick, he had been a nurse for 30 years and still exhibited a tremendous capacity to serve others.

I had the opportunity to interview him for an article for our health system newsletter. It was then that I realized how he gave of himself wholeheartedly and never experienced a minute of compassion fatigue. When asked how he kept on giving and giving, he explained:

"First of all, caring for others is one of my core values. I was raised with that value, and then I practice it with a partner who also values compassionate caring. We actually met at a volunteer event. We worked on a committee together and we both realized at the same time that we shared many common interests and thoughts about life. We have been together for ten years and everyday is an adventure. We make thoughtful decisions as a team as to where we want to put our time. We both work full time so we have to choose wisely. Additionally, I care for myself in the same manner I care for others. I know myself and when I start to feel stressed or needing some downtime, I either go to the gym and work out or I go outside for long, fast walks. These activities fill me up and I'm able to be present for my partner and go out into my community and give some more."

Frederick has found the key to avoiding compassion fatigue in his three well-taken points:

• He has a life partner who validates him in both his work as a nurse and in his work as a volunteer.

• He and his partner choose where to put their time. They make a decision as opposed to feeling guilty, meeting the expectations of others or an inability to say no. Their choices give them great joy.

• He has learned the value of authentic, sustainable self-care. He knows what fills him up (i.e., workouts and walking) and understands the rewards of caring for himself.

Frederick's story does not indicate that these fortunate folks who understand healthy caregiving lack compassion or empathy. Nor does it mean they are stronger, smarter, or better suited to a caregiving profession than those of us prone to suffer the symptoms. It means that those who do not fall into the shoals of compassion fatigue understand and put into practice the self-directed care necessary for a happy, healthy, productive life. Self-directed care includes such notions as happy, healthy relationships, well-defined personal boundaries, self-awareness, and application of practical life coping skills.

Many of us who are at-risk for compassion fatigue failed to learn the art of self-care, weren't fortunate to have mandatory life coping skills modeled for us and possibly never witnessed happy, healthy relationships. Often, those of us dedicated to caregiving aren't even aware of our own symptoms, let alone that a blueprint exists for healthy self-preservation.

In the past, as a single mother of three children, working two stressful jobs to make ends meet, I basically ran on empty 100% of the time. My health suffered, as did all of my relationships. Feelings of isolation, sadness, and just plain bone-tiredness were present year after year. I didn't know I was experiencing classic compassion fatigue symptoms and, more important, I didn't know that my symptoms could be managed in order to create a better life for me and my children.

Young students, family caregivers, those re-entering the workforce and, of course, those already working in the helping professions, will benefit simply from an awareness of compassion fatigue and what it represents. It is never too late to cultivate and apply self-directed care that nourishes and sustains all of our resources – mental, physical and spiritual. I was in my early 50's when I began to seriously incorporate a model of positive self-care into my life. It is true that we don't know what we've got until we lose it. But it is also true that we don't know what we've been missing until it arrives.

Try to remember, also, that a little humor goes a long way. We caregivers tend to be a very serious lot, not only about ourselves, but our work as well. And rightly so. There is nothing funny about watching a child die of cancer, or diagnosing a patient with schizophrenia, or watching a perfectly wonderful kitten being euthanized simply because there isn't one more cage available in the shelter. We know now that humor can, and does, absorb some of the trauma that leads to compassion fatigue. Back in the 1970's, a popular television series called *M.A.S.H.* invited viewers to experience war up close and personal. M.A.S.H. stood for Mobile Army Surgical Hospital. The tents, set up on the Korean War battlefield, served as operating rooms for those maimed and injured on the front lines. While the gallows or black humor unnerved us, the reality of the situation was not lost. The glib, often caustic, banter between the surgeons, nurses, and patients lightened everyone's gruesome load. The fast-paced repartee also served as a bonding mechanism for those involved.

As you begin to recognize and understand the effect humor can have on alleviating compassion fatigue, you will find examples popping up everywhere. At this writing, *SCRUBS* and *Grey's Anatomy*, two popular TV shows, rely heavily on the same type of comedic relief as young interns navigate the harrowing world of hospitals. Keep in mind that a well-placed comment, followed by a hardy belly laugh, can lift our spirits and allow us to continue with the caregiving work at hand.

Writer Doris Lessing offers the following: Laughter is, by definition, healthy.

So let's get on with it. Below, you will find the Professional Quality of Life Scale Self-Test, scoring instructions and descriptions that will be useful in helping to determine your own level of compassion fatigue, if it does indeed exist. This Quality of Life Self-Test is the work of Dr. Beth Hudnall-Stamm, a professor at the Institute of Rural Health at Idaho State University in Pocatello, Idaho.

Take time answering and scoring the questions. Sections include Compassion Satisfaction, which is about the pleasure you derive from your work; Burnout; which helps measure feelings associated with hopelessness and difficulties; and Compassion Fatigue/Secondary Trauma, which chronicles your work-related, secondary exposure to stressful events. Pay particular attention to the debriefing at the end of the test as the information will help you to understand how the results apply to you personally. There are no right or wrong answers, only truthful ones.

ProQOL R-IV SELF-TEST

PROFESSIONAL QUALITY OF LIFE SCALE
Compassion Satisfaction and Fatigue Subscales—Revision IV

[Helping] people puts you in direct contact with their lives. As you probably have experienced, your compassion for those you *[help]* has both positive and negative aspects. We would like to ask you questions about your experiences, both positive and negative, as a *[helper]*. Consider each of the following questions about you and your current situation. Select the number that honestly reflects how frequently you experienced these characteristics in the **_last 30 days_**.

0 = Never   1 = Rarely 2 = A Few Times 3 = Somehwat Often
4 = Often   5 = Very Often

_____ 1.   I am happy.

_____ 2.   I am preoccupied with more than one person I *[help]*.

_____ 3.   I get satisfaction from being able to *[help]* people.

_____ 4.   I feel connected to others.

_____ 5.   I jump or am startled by unexpected sounds.

_____ 6.   I feel invigorated after working with those I *[help]*.

_____ 7. I find it difficult to separate my personal life from my life as a *[helper]*.

_____ 8. I'm losing sleep over traumatic experiences of a person I *[help]*.

_____ 9. I think that I might have been "infected" by the traumatic stress of those I *[help]*.

_____ 10. I feel trapped by my work as a *[helper]*.

_____ 11. Because of my *[helping]*, I have felt "on edge" about various things.

_____ 12. I like my work as a *[helper]*.

_____ 13. I feel depressed as a result of my work as a *[helper]*.

_____ 14. I feel as though I am experiencing the trauma of someone I have *[helped]*.

_____ 15. I have beliefs that sustain me.

_____ 16. I am pleased with how I am able to keep up with *[helping]* techniques and protocols.

_____ 17. I am the person I always wanted to be.

_____ 18. My work makes me feel satisfied.

_____ 19. Because of my work as a *[helper]*, I feel exhausted.

_____ 20. I have happy thoughts and feelings about those I *[help]* and how I could help them.

_____ 21. I feel overwhelmed by the amount of work or the size of my case*[work]*load I have to deal with.

_____ 22. I believe I can make a difference through my work.

_____ 23. I avoid certain activities or situations because they remind me of frightening experiences of the people I *[help]*.

_____ 24. I am proud of what I can do to *[help]*.

_____ 25. As a result of my *[helping]*, I have intrusive, frightening thoughts.

_____ 26. I feel "bogged down" by the system.

_____ 27.   I have thoughts that I am a "success" as a *[helper]*.

_____ 28.   I can't recall important parts of my work with trauma victims.

_____ 29.   I am a very sensitive person.

_____ 30.   I am happy that I chose to do this work.

_____   **TOTAL**

Self-scoring directions, if used as self-test:

1. Be certain you respond to all items.
2. On some items the scores need to be reversed. Next to your response write the reverse of that score (i.e. 0=0, 1=5, 2=4, 3=3). Reverse the scores on these 5 items: 1, 4, 15, 17 and 29. Please note that the value 0 is not reversed, as its value is always null.
3. Mark the items for scoring:
    a. Put an **X** by the 10 items that form the **Compassion Satisfaction Scale**: 3, 6, 12, 16, 18, 20, 22, 24, 27, 30.
    b. Put a **check** by the 10 items on the **Burnout Scale**: 1, 4, 8, 10, 15, 17, 19, 21, 26, 29.
    c. **Circle** the 10 items on the **Trauma/Compassion Fatigue Scale**: 2, 5, 7, 9, 11, 13, 14, 23, 25, 28.
4. Add the numbers you wrote next to the items for each set of items and compare with the following scoring grid:

Compassion Satisfaction: This part of the test is about the pleasure you derive from being able to do your work well. Higher scores on this scale represent a greater satisfaction related to your ability to be an effective caregiver in your job.

> **Scoring:** The average score is 37. About 25% of people score higher than 42 and about 25% of people score below 33. If you scored in the higher range, you most likely derive a good deal of professional satisfaction from your work. If your score is below 33, you may not derive satisfaction from your job.

Burnout: Associated with feelings of hopelessness and difficulties in dealing with work or doing the job effectively, burnout is a gradual process. The negative emotions reflect the feelings that your efforts make no difference, or they can be associated with a heavy workload and/or a non-supportive work environment.

> **Scoring:** The average score is 22. About 25% of people score above 27 and about 25% of people score below 18. If you scored below 18, you probably have positive feelings of being effective in your job. If you scored above 22, you may be harboring negative emotions about your job. If high scores persist, it might be a call to re-examine your motives for remaining in your job.

Compassion Fatigue/Secondary Trauma: This portion is related to Vicarious Traumatization (VT), which is about your work-related exposure to extremely stressful events. If you are constantly witnessing the trauma of others, you are experiencing secondary exposure. The symptoms of CF/STS (Secondary Traumatic Stress) are usually rapid in onset and associated with a particular event. Symptoms include: being afraid, difficulty sleeping, and reoccurring disturbing images.

> **Scoring:** The average score on this scale is 13. About 25% of people score below 8 and about 25% of people score above 17. Higher scores may indicate the need to examine how you feel about your work and your work environment.

(Taken from the ProQOL Manual by Dr. Beth Hudnall-Stamm)

Copyright Information

Disclaimer

☀

※

CHAPTER THREE: BURDENS OF THE CHOSEN

"The price one pays for pursuing any profession or

calling is an intimate knowledge of its ugly side.

– James Baldwin

If it has been established that caring too much can hurt, why do some caregivers suffer the symptoms associated with compassion fatigue and others don't? And why, if compassion fatigue is present, are some caregivers able to successfully manage their symptoms, while others cannot?

These questions lead us to the heart of this chapter: What are the root causes of compassion fatigue?

Unfortunately, the answers to those often-asked questions above aren't simple. While researchers have been able to help us understand what compassion fatigue looks like and how to manage its symptoms, there is no definitive way to know, at least outwardly, who is at-risk and who isn't. What we do know is this: Due to the distinct nature of caregiving and its inherent ability to challenge our belief systems and change who we are, the possibility of experiencing compassion fatigue lies within every caregiver. This is particularly true of psychiatrists and psychologists working with clients suffering from the ravages of betrayal and violence trauma where the stories can be highly personal and painful. Whether or not we develop the full-blown symptoms, or as Baldwin suggests in the opening quote, intimately become acquainted with its ugly side, depends on a number of factors.

Studies show that those of us at-risk or suffering from compassion fatigue are most likely "other-directed." Simply put, we fill the needs of others before, or instead of, filling our own needs.

I once witnessed a heart-wrenching case of total self-neglect by a mother and daughter at a workshop I presented for a general audience. The three-hour course was open to anyone who wanted to learn more about compassion fatigue. At the beginning of the morning session, each member of the group was asked to introduce herself, why she was attending and what she hoped to bring out of the workshop. The first three participants were professionals who knew of compassion fatigue and thought, perhaps, they were heading down that road. Then we came to Joanna and Joy (not their real names), a mother and daughter team. Daughter Joy spoke for the two of them. Mother Joanna sat quietly with her head down while Joy offered the following story:

> *"My mom and I love animals. We take in all of the stray cats in our city. Then we have them spayed or neutered, have their shots, get them licensed and then try to find good homes for them. Right now, we have 35 cats in our three-bedroom house. We've run into a problem now and don't know what to do. We have maxed out our credit cards, our savings, sold many of our family treasures, and even had to sell our car to feed and care for the cats. The bank is threatening to foreclose on our house because we haven't been able to pay the mortgage for the past three months. I work full time, but my salary doesn't come close to covering our expenses, let alone the expenses for caring for the cats. We love all these animals and if we don't take care of them, who will? If we lose our home, where will all of these little cats go?"*

Joy presented the most extreme case of "other-directedness" that I've seen in my compassion fatigue work. It was obvious that boundaries were blurred and that neither mother nor daughter comprehended where they left off and the stray cats began. I believe her last statement was the most telling: *If we lose our home, where will all of these little cats go?* In this statement, there is a complete disregard for her welfare or that of her mother. The only concern is the stray cats. It was obvious right from the beginning that there was nothing I could do to help this unfortunate situation. I recommended they locate some professional help as soon as possible. Their local shelter would most likely be a good place to start.

Your story hopefully isn't this severe. But were there elements of the story that rang a bell? If anything sounded familiar to you, it is likely that you have not practiced healthy self-care in a while, if ever. And this has placed excessive burdens on you, your life and your loved ones. To better understand your tendency towards compassion fatigue, you may need to delve into your past and examine if, and how, you've dealt with personal boundaries throughout your life. Most likely, you haven't been as protective of yourself and your resources as you now need to be. Depending on how extensively you've abandoned your own needs, this process may be difficult and painful.

The most powerful contributor to compassion fatigue stems from the perceptions and realities we carry within us from childhood experiences. As we mature and our personalities become more complex, myriad childhood memories shape our attitudes, ideals and values, which in turn have manifested as behaviors and habits. If secure, loving and validating experiences were plentiful in our formative years, we have the potential to become open, optimistic, well-adjusted caregivers. If our childhood was fraught with dysfunction such as addictions, abuse or untreated mental illnesses, the possibility of developing compassion fatigue or other maladies certainly multiplies. As we age, additional unfavorable life experiences can add to an already explosive arsenal of painful memories.

An elderly woman attended one of my community compassion fatigue workshops. During the workshop, she told her story about the losses she suffered as a child and how the patterns of pain and suffering they caused continue to overwhelm her today. This is her unusual story:

"I was born in London. I was a young child when World War II broke out. My family lived on a beautiful estate as my father was a prosperous banker. We were very well respected in our community. I remember the sirens and the bombs falling as if it were yesterday. Our family home was bombed and fire devastated the grounds. We had nowhere to go – nowhere to turn. We moved into the country home of an aunt. Their home was already crowded as they had seven children of their own and when you added the five members of my family, we overflowed. We were, of course, grateful, but we considered ourselves refugees.

Eventually, after the war, my family stayed in London and I immigrated to the United States. I continued to send money home to help support my parents and my siblings. My mother died when I was only 20 years old and to this day, I grieve the fact that she never knew my children and now my grandchildren. When each one of my three children left home to go to college, I continued to grieve for what I had lost. Three years ago, when my beloved dog and cat died within two weeks of each other, I was devastated. I am barely surviving this new loss."

It is quite possible that she suffers from compassion fatigue along with traumatic stress she has been carrying for more than sixty years. More important is the fact that the horrific loss and trauma she suffered as a child continues to plague her today. She suffers a number of physical ailments, most of which are unnamed and chronic. As she ages, joy and happiness elude her much of the time.

Within the process of learning to recognize and manage compassion fatigue is the potential to "clean out" the cobwebs of our early painful experiences that hold us hostage and sap our life energies. If we continue to ward off the pain within, eventually our bodies rebel and ill-health sets in. What doesn't move through us, defines us.

While the majority of our early childhood stories are nowhere near as traumatic as that of my friend, it is important to note that well-meaning, loving parents are capable of wounding the hearts and spirits of their children. While negative reactions such as blaming and punishing are meant to be life lessons, these actions can bruise or crush a child's feelings of self-worth and acceptability. In her book, *"Healing the Sensitive Heart: How to Stop Getting Hurt, Build Your Inner Strength, and Find The Love You Deserve,"* psychologist Debra Mandel writes:

> *"There are as many varieties of psychological mistreatment as there are cereals on the market shelves. Here, too, what might be inconsequential behavior for one child might be devastating to another. Some of the most potentially wounding forms of psychological abuse include name-calling, threatening of abandonment, deprivation or physical violence, intentional humiliation, shame or ridicule, blame, and/or devaluing a child's expressed interests, needs and desires."*

Leading traumatologist Dr. J. Eric Gentry agrees with this statement when he offers that, as a species, we haven't yet been able to raise our children without harming them.

As a reader, you may take umbrage at the above statements. After all, you may feel you had loving, caring parents who did the best they could to give you every possible opportunity to develop into a caring, loving human being. It is at this intersection with the information you are about to read that you may begin to feel uncomfortable and insecure. This is certainly normal when approaching new ideas that challenge former beliefs and have the potential to literally change who we are.

As you continue on in this chapter, I ask that you remain open and curious. The data presented is universal and in no way personal. If asked to explore your familial customs, cultures, traditions or rituals, no lack of respect is intended. Interpreting these markers in relation to the causes of compassion fatigue will only serve to clarify and, ultimately, strengthen your understanding and awareness. In turn, this will help you to combat compassion fatigue in your own helping career, as well as recognize it in others and assist them in their healing process.

The Arizona Center for Social Trauma website (www.acst-international.com) lists strategies for prevention of compassion fatigue. All are noteworthy but one suggestion is imperative if we hope to avoid the distressing symptoms: Fearlessly examine and re-examine your helping and caregiving motivations.

And that is what we are about to do.

In France, there is a saying: *Nous allons en arrière, amèliorer le saut.* That is, we go backwards, to better jump. As we proceed to explore the "burden" we now label compassion fatigue, this is certainly the case. Returning to our formative years and reflecting on how our emotional and psychological patterns emerged is the first step in this journey. While this process takes time and patience, it is undoubtedly the best way to gauge our candidacy for compassion fatigue today and in the future. Some of the ideas presented might evoke feelings of sadness or nostalgia. Some of the information might resonate in a way that makes you uncomfortable, perhaps even a little angry or resentful. Remember, what you feel is what you feel. Experiencing a range of feelings is perfectly normal.

Once I had an animal control officer in a workshop. He made it quite clear from the beginning that he was only there because it was mandatory. His boss directed him to attend. While the other members of the group showed great interest in the concept of compassion fatigue, he continued to let out loud sighs, repeatedly asked when the next break was coming and basically refused to take part in any of the exercises. I felt I had to bring him into the conversation. Due to the nature of his job, there was a good possibility he had developed compassion fatigue symptoms. After lunch, I asked him specifically how he was able to handle the stress of his job. He answered:

> *"I don't find my job stressful at all. It's what I do. The other day, I got a call from a motorist who had just hit a deer. She was hysterical on the phone and said the deer was badly hurt, but bounced off her car and ran off. I got the directions and headed out that way. There was a large field and I figured I could find the deer on foot. I grabbed my gun, left my truck and walked across the field. It didn't take long before I found the deer. It was lying on the ground, half dead from the accident. Didn't bother me at all. I took my gun and pointed it right between its eyes and shot. Didn't bother me at all. It's my job. I can handle it"*

The gasp from the other participants was audible. I passed the Kleenex around and stood by the animal control officer. I asked the simple question: Why do you think it doesn't bother you? He hemmed a bit and repeatedly shook his head from side to side. The longer he sat there quietly, the more his eyes filled with tears. Soon he was crying along with the rest of us.

Simply put, a caring human being can't do a job like his and not feel emotions. He had pushed his feelings down so far that he thought they were non-existent. My guess is the workshop was the first time he actually thought about the incident and processed the emotions attached to the trauma he experienced. When he left, he thanked me and said he was going to rethink what he was doing for a living and think about changing jobs – at least for a while.

We never know who or what circumstances will trigger painful memories. The stimulus can be first-hand, such as involvement in an abusive relationship, or second-hand, such as listening to a client relay harrowing tales of pain and loss. However the situation presents itself, the hurting surfaces immediately and stings. Eventually, if the root of the powerful reaction isn't examined and healed, we learn to protect ourselves in a number of unhealthy ways. In turn, these unhealthy habits such as substance abuse, lashing out in anger, self-inflicting wounds and other forms of emotional and behavioral abuse will eventually manifest as illness throughout the physical body.

If we have not developed well-defined personal boundaries, genuine feelings of self-worth and healthy communication skills, we will do whatever it takes to alleviate the distressing emotions. This can mean isolating ourselves from others or becoming reliant on others to meet our most basic needs. Or worst of all, just stuffing the painful emotions down so deep that we naively believe they no longer exist.

We can all probably name someone who uses one or more of these behaviors to protect his or herself - perhaps a friend who explodes at the slightest provocation. We often call these people "hotheads," or say they have a short fuse. Road rage is a prime example of how emotional issues that have not been dealt with effectively spill over and erupt at an inappropriate time. Perhaps you have a sibling who recoils in social situations and prefers a computer to people, seeming much like a turtle in a shell. We label these people "introverts" or "nerds." Or perhaps you have an elderly relative who doesn't seem to have much reaction to his or her surroundings. We tend to say that these people have "checked out." Maybe you even recognize some of these behaviors in yourself.

In my work with non-profit organizations where compassion fatigue is rampant, I can honestly say I've worked with colleagues who display all of the behaviors above. In Chapter Eight where we will take a look at organizational compassion fatigue, it will become very clear that the majority of people who enter helping professions do not take the time to do what you are doing now – examining their caregiving motives. The result is, pure and simple, disastrous. These folks, no matter how good hearted they may be, bring all of their pain, sadness, loss, and fear right into the workplace, and if you befriend them, right into your life.

It is certainly understandable why most of us make sweeping attempts to avoid emotional earthquakes. When someone makes a hurtful remark or chooses to reject or abandon us, it takes great skill and awareness to keep the lines of communication open and deliver a calm response. Most of us don't welcome pain and suffering into our lives even though both are integral aspects of the human experience. If we see it coming, we run the other way as fast as our legs can carry us. Unfortunately, lashing out, isolation, and stuffing emotions only serves to damage our growth and potential and aids in the construction of a psychological fortress better known as denial.

I have found in both myself and working with others recovering from compassion fatigue that denial is the most insidious symptom. When we deny the presence of feelings where pain, suffering, and trauma exist, we are basically denying our humanity. It is far more satisfying to activate our lachrymal glands via tears of joy rather than tears of sadness. But, in a sense, we *are* our feelings. As children, if we are allowed to express and demonstrate the wide range of normal human emotions – joy, fear, sadness, pain, loss, happiness, anger – chances are in our favor that we will develop into an integrated being with a sense of wholeness.

Unfortunately, many of us learned at a very early age to bury our feelings in order to show strength, detachment or personal power. Often burying feelings was a way of sustaining family secrets such as alcoholism or sexual addiction.

A young woman in one of my workshops worked as a social worker. During the introductions, I asked each participant to share what he or she does to decompress. When it came to this particular young woman, she said she liked to write poetry. When I asked what her favorite subject was to write about, she answered: dogs. As the workshop continued, she shared with the group that she was raised in a highly dysfunctional family that suffered the ravages of both alcoholism and physical abuse. As she told her story, her sadness and loneliness was palpable. She finished her story by telling us that the reason she writes poems about dogs is because it was her little dog Josie who offered her consolation and security as a child when her world raged around her. She said: I had to be strong to survive in my family, I couldn't show my feelings of anger, sadness or fear. Now, as an adult, those feelings still live inside of me. I let them out and tame them by writing love poems to dogs to honor Josie for saving my life.

As we age, if we don't process childhood pain in a manner such as this intelligent young woman, a pattern of denial becomes an intrinsic part of our personality. Not only do we excel at voiding a huge part of ourselves, we take pride in it. The fragmentation that occurs continues to erode our well-being until one day, something catastrophic happens and we have to face that part of ourselves that we have denied - that place where all of the pain and suffering resides. This dark side is often referred to as our "shadow."

Author Sharon Salzberg in her book *Lovingkindness: The Revolutionary Art of Happiness*, sums it up this way:

> *"Our vision becomes very narrow when we need things to be a certain way and cannot accept things the way they actually are. Denial functions almost as a kind of narcotic, so that vital parts of us end up missing."*

Of course, as with everything in life, there are two sides of the story. Denial can be very useful by providing protection from stressful reality and giving us time to adjust to a new reality. Indeed, denial has been found to be a major factor in mitigating highly stressful events such as the death of a spouse (Figley, 1999). While this form of denial is short-lived, the form of denial that has potential to become compassion fatigue is present in the individual long term.

If the assault on our emotions becomes repetitive, as it does when working in many caregiving professions, many of us will turn to drugs, alcohol, food, tobacco, or similar addictive methods to soothe the pain. Sadly, addictions add momentum to the downward spiral that deadens emotions entirely. The longer we continue to distance ourselves emotionally, the more detached and fragmented our personalities become. Once disintegration of the self occurs, we are no longer attached to the authenticity that makes each one of us a unique and valuable individual. This spiral also robs us of the energy we need to achieve our dreams. Determination, dedication and self-discipline are no longer present to assist in motivating us to do well.

The interesting thing is that no matter what we do or say, that empty hole that should have been filled with love, care and understanding during our formative years, is now filled with resentment, pain, anger, feelings of loneliness and abandonment.

If we face these demons, all of the fears and anxieties that have been accumulating and growing out of proportion over the years will surface. Is it any wonder why humans chose to deny the reality of that dreary inner space and chose to suppress or deny its existence?

The problem with suppressing and denying is this: It is in that place of pain, loneliness and feelings of abandonment that compassion fatigue takes hold and leads to unhealthy caregiving practices and processes.

Many popular authors such as Alice Sebold and Ellen Waterston have shared their experiences with these harmful patterns of negating emotions and the fallout associated with years of denial. In their books *Lucky* and *Then There Was No Mountain: The Parallel Odyssey of a Mother and Daughter Through Addiction*, respectively, both authors examine how detrimental it is to wellness to suppress past traumas and pain.

Alice Sebold was raped and beaten as an 18-year-old Syracuse University student. By her own account, the trauma created such pain and grief that she sunk into a 9-year quagmire of alcohol, heroin, and sexual addiction before seeking help and, ultimately, recovery. Ellen Waterston's flight from emotional and behavioral addictions, denial, and guilt wrought by her family of origin was brought about when she staged an intervention to save her embittered, addicted 16-year-old daughter. In the end, both mother and daughter chose healing and recovery.

As in the stories of both of these courageous writers, we are all capable of choosing to heal and recover. But before we get to that decision-making point, we must be able to recognize when, and if, we are choosing denial as a means of self-protection and survival. When the level of pain, grief, and loss are within a modest range, it is much easier to recognize when some level of denial is at work in our lives. We take the time to dig deep and uncover a core, even if it means working through some tough stuff. This process frees us from repeating damaging patterns over and over again. Or at least if we do repeat a pattern and fall into a hole, we are able to pull ourselves out and start all over again. But we now know that it doesn't take severe abuse or other family dysfunction to wound the human spirit and create cause for denial. Writer John Steinbeck once commented, "To be alive at all, is to have scars."

At this time, let's revisit the idea of childhood wounding.

As a species, we have not yet learned how to raise our children without hurting them. At a training session when I first heard traumatologist J. Eric Gentry, PhD, make that statement, I found myself disagreeing wholeheartedly. Having been raised by hardworking parents whose number one mission in life was to provide well for their four children, that statement made no sense whatsoever. But as he continued and explained the profound effect our negative childhood experiences have on our propensity for experiencing compassion fatigue, I began to open myself up to this new idea. He suggested that even the most involved, loving, committed parents can display behaviors or speak negative words that can scar their children. And quite possibly, the parents are completely unaware how this negativity imprints their offspring. If for no other reason, the parents are unaware that they are modeling patterns which are familiar; the same patterns present in their formative years.

Unfortunately, society as a whole doesn't help. Researchers are now uncovering the psychological and emotional damage children suffer due to unkind, malicious classmates, bullies, teachers, coaches, and others residing in that village that it takes to raise a child. Most likely, there is not a human being alive who hasn't been wounded or hurt in some way. Obviously, the extent of the damage varies depending on how severe the trauma. In her book *Secrets, Lies, Betrayals: How the Body Holds the Secrets of a Life, and How to Unlock Them*, psychologist Maggie Scarf points out that early traumas don't have to be Big Time, such as sexual, physical, or verbal abuse to make an indelible mark on a child. Trauma can arise from situations as simple as always being the last one chosen for a team, or a young girl being called "bird legs" on the way to school by a gang of mischievous boys.

It isn't easy to admit that we didn't receive enough attention, validation, love, warmth, physical contact, stimulation, or support while we were growing up. Why? Because we know in our hearts and minds that we can't go back. That time is gone, never to return. This is especially true if we've come to the realization that our parents did the best they could with the knowledge, skills and resources they had. But that realization doesn't help to diminish the simple truth that if, indeed, we perceive a void where love, security, or validation should have been, we are going to manifest or act out in order to get what we didn't get, and more important, what we continue to need.

We do not grow out of what we lacked. We carry that inner void with us. It is in this inner void that compassion fatigue flourishes.

Author Antwone Fisher wrote a poem entitled *Who Will Cry for the Little Boy?* This poignant prose recalls his lonely childhood in foster care where he experienced abuse and neglect. The first and last stanzas describe the feeling associated with carrying the void within. While his story is one of pain and suffering, his words speak for all of us to some degree. He wrote the poem at age 43.

Who will cry for the little boy?
Lost and all alone.
Who will cry for the little boy?
Abandoned without his own?

Who will cry for the little boy?
A good boy he tried to be.
Who will cry for the little boy?
Who cries inside of me.

Fisher has a profound awareness of the little boy who cries inside of him – now a mature, grown man. While honoring the memory of that little boy, he also appears mindful that the little boy holds a tremendous power to recreate the pain, grief, suffering and loss he endured as a child. Perhaps it was years of therapy that helped Fisher to accept, grieve and move beyond his abusive childhood to become a successful, productive human being. Since many of us don't seek professional help and haven't the tools to explore these deep, dark crevices of our existence, what happens to our "inner" child who might be crying out? How does that child make his or herself known? How does that inner child seek validation?

If, as children, we perceived or actually experienced a lack of love, care, support, validation or security, and haven't taken responsibility for meeting our own needs as adults, we will continue to look to fill those elusive needs outside of ourselves. We will seek what we lack in others, in our acquisition of material things, in addictive substances such as food, alcohol, drugs, and any other device that we believe offers us solace, comfort and escape.

Some of us seek what we lack in giving care to others. By showing kindness and compassion to others, we are emulating a giving pattern we so desperately crave in our own lives, but haven't yet received. In essence, we are modeling our wants and desires. And more important, if our own pain and trauma are only one step outside of our consciousness, we leave ourselves open to absorbing the pain and trauma of the person in our care. It is a perfect union: Their pain and suffering connects with our pain and suffering and produces a secondary traumatic stress reaction. We re-live our sorrows in the presence of another sorrow-filled human being. If this occurs on a continuous basis, such as in a day to day caregiving job, imagine the toll it takes on the caregiver!

We human beings not only connect with other suffering human beings, but abused or abandoned animals as well. Tami L. Harbolt wrote a book entitled *Bridging the Bond: The Cultural Construction of the Shelter Pet.* In this highly acclaimed study, she not only explores the psychology of the shelter animals, but the shelter workers as well. While her venue is the animal shelter, her observations arguably apply to any caregiving environment. She writes:

> *"My personal experiences working in an animal shelter for the past several years have led me to believe that people are drawn to sheltering work out of more than simply a desire to help the animals. Many of the people I met in this community had experienced various forms of oppression, either in a familial, societal, or biological way. This experience of oppression led many of these workers and volunteers to develop a heightened empathy for animals, based on the perceived experience of shared oppression".*

Karen W. Saavkvitne and Laurie Anne Pearlman recant this theme in *Transforming the Pain: A Workbook on Vicarious Traumatization* in discussing the relationship of trauma worker to client:

> *"The imagery that plagues an individual (the caregiver) will often reflect the psychological needs that are most important to him or her. Thus when we are tormented by a particular story, it usually echoes something specific about our own needs and beliefs that has been challenged or activated, as well as something about our relationship with the client and the client's unique history and story".*

Author Harbolt adds to that concept and takes it a step further:

"I will suggest in this book that people are drawn to animal shelter and welfare work because it is highly dramatic, intense, and characterized by joyful highs and overwhelming setbacks. And it satisfies some need in people not only to control their social environments, but also to rearrange their legacies of disenfranchisement".

Writer Ellen Glasgow in her memoir *The Woman Within* suggests the same sentiment in a simpler statement. She wrote: "The heart, once broken, appears to be forever looking for trouble of the same nature." If what she wrote is true, and we continue as adults to harbor our childhood sorrows mindlessly in denial, we are doomed to attract the same situations that allow the same feelings to take hold. We do so, unaware, in hopes of affecting a different outcome; an outcome that satisfies our unmet needs.

I once worked with a very likeable young man whom I'll call John. While it was obvious he possessed tremendous talents in the area of graphic design, he labored in an entry level animal caregiving position, received minimum wage and found numerous ways to avoid doing the job he was hired to do. When he wasn't complaining about his persistent headache, low-grade fever or his chronic sinus infection, he faulted management for not listening to his ideas, which he was sure would improve both the flow and processes of the shelter.

As you've probably guessed, John was chronically under-employed and suffered from high levels of compassion fatigue. His symptoms were exacerbated by the fact that he also suffered from burnout, which appeared to be due to the fact that he had been in unsatisfying, unchallenging jobs for several years. Despite all of the forces working against him, John displayed natural leadership qualities. He was often found holding court with mesmerized co-workers who, upon listening to his tirades, agreed that the shelter was, indeed, a horrible place to work. When the productivity of the group severely declined, management stepped in. As the trainer, I was asked to take John aside several times a week to work on his communication skills. His manager believed that honing John's listening and speaking skills might help him to present himself more effectively, thus allowing his good ideas to be heard and validated. If given the proper tools to help manage his compassion fatigue and burnout, perhaps he could affect positive changes in the workplace.

The first few sessions with John went very well. I learned that he had left his home in Alabama at the age of 17, without the benefit of his high school diploma. While "on the road" for two years, he worked at menial jobs in order to feed himself and finally landed in California where he decided to put down roots. When I asked about family, he winced slightly and said he hadn't seen or heard from anyone in a number of years. A fact he found comforting since his background was mired in alcohol and domestic abuse – an unfriendly place where no one valued his input, validated his ideas or respected his judgment.

We then focused on his uncanny ability to affect others in both his actions and his words. He began to understand that he could, and did, affect those around him and that it would serve him well to take responsibility for his untamed personal power. We discussed the idea of containing rumors and gossip as a way of building morale and trust between staff and management. He suggested leading a "stop smoking" campaign (many of the staff members were heavy smokers), and perhaps organizing an after work bowling tournament to bolster team spirit. I felt we were making progress and that he was well on his way to grasping the concept of compassion fatigue and how the symptoms were intruding on his life. It wasn't until he made an interesting comment that I realized we had only scratched the surface as to what was really going on.

"I love my job," he admitted one afternoon, "but I hate coming to work every morning."

It took me a few seconds to digest John's comment. How could he love his job and hate it at the same time? Since John's potential wasn't being tapped in his current job and his innate talents and skills were not being utilized, I guessed he was simply unhappy in the work environment. That would certainly explain why he hated coming to work. When I asked why he didn't give notice at the shelter, return to school and study the disciplines in which he excelled, his reply provided a glimpse into a much bigger issue.

"I guess the reason I don't want to leave this place," he expressed sadly, "is because everyone here is so much like family."

Everyone here is so much like family. No wonder he was always at the center of the workplace dramas! He was on that fragmented emotional roller coaster ride that was churning up feelings of chaos and confusion. He was experiencing the confusion inherent when competing perceptions create emotional conflicts. John did love his job. He had a passion for helping animals and he felt the work he was doing made a difference, if not for all of society's unwanted, abused or neglected animals, at least for those in his care. When I asked John what specifically he didn't like about his job, he replied "constantly butting heads with management." The source of those chronic headaches suddenly became crystal clear! When asked how he viewed his management team, he replied, "They don't value my input, validate my ideas, or respect my judgment." The comment mirrored his assessment of why he left his family at age 17.

John's story serves as an example of how we often deliver

our past right into our present, often completely unaware and in denial. We keep creating the same situations over and over and over again, only the details differ. John truly believed that leaving Georgia and being away from his family changed who he was. In some regard, it did. He physically removed himself, became more self-sufficient and independent. What he failed to see was that the little boy from Alabama continued to live inside of him.

Physicist Albert Einstein made the statement that problems cannot be solved with the same awareness that created them. John presented the perfect model for that sentiment. Once he understood the negative patterning that was keeping him mired in compassion fatigue symptoms, he was able to let go of the outmoded attitudes, self-defeating behaviors and unreasonable expectations that he had placed on himself. He realized he could not "fix" his family of origin. Once he released himself from that task, it no longer held power over him. Needless to say, his aches and pains disappeared. He began to recognize that the only power he could wield in changing his past was to change his future. Psychologist and Holocaust survivor Victor Frankl reminds us that when we are no longer able to change a situation, we are challenged to change ourselves.

Thus, the need to change becomes the burden of the chosen. As anyone knows who has tried to change habits, thoughts or attitudes, change is a process that takes time, energy, awareness, mindfulness, and commitment. There is much we can do to actually change our brains to think and react differently. These changes or shifts take patience and an understanding of what is happening. Once the shifts occur, they alter the way we see our world. There is no magic involved. We just begin to have better choices, and subsequently, better lives.

When putting our own needs on hold in order to fulfill the needs of others becomes our standard mode of existence – our lifestyle, our way of life – there will be fallout. That fallout is compassion fatigue. The severity of the symptoms will be gauged by how far we've strayed from the authentic self. It is in that loss of self where our unmet needs collide with outmoded family patterns, self-defeating behaviors and painful memories that the psychological, emotional, and physical damage will manifest.

The good news for caregivers is that it is possible to work through these issues successfully and create a healthy, vibrant life. Poet Roger Housden, in his most wonderful book *Ten Poems to Change Your Life*, says it best: The heart, like a grape, is prime to deliver its harvest in the same moment that it appears to be crushed.

What we will uncover in the next chapter is that it is possible to make the decision to heal. And in doing so, we open ourselves up to receive one of life's unexpected rewards – the ability to turn our greatest pain into our greatest pleasure; taking the cause and turning it into the cure. We begin to give care from a place of abundance as opposed to a place of depletion.

*

✳

CHAPTER FOUR: THE DECISION TO HEAL

Healing is a very personal experience. We all have our own way of dealing with physical or emotional pain, a broken bone or a broken heart. Some of us prefer to share every last detail of our misery with others; some of us prefer to suffer in silence. For some, physical activity such as swimming, biking, hiking, or mountain climbing aids in healing. For others, a quiet walk in the woods works wonders.

With compassion fatigue, the decision to heal is often not a decision at all, but a necessity. If the symptoms of compassion fatigue have surfaced in ways that are distressing and depressing the life of a caregiver, the only way out is to make a conscious decision to heal. Eating well, sleeping well, and exercising certainly go a long way in lessening the symptoms of compassion fatigue. But there is only one way to truly manage the disruptive symptoms and break the cycle of re-wounding. *That way is to heal from the inside out.* We must travel deep within where patterns of internal conflict and broken-ness continue to play out. In short, we must embrace and then heal the core of our pain. It is imperative that we learn to weep for a stranger, and then be able to walk away, stronger and stable instead of weakened and wobbly!

Anyone who has experienced the excruciating emotional pain that compassion fatigue brings on understands what the great philosopher Plato was thinking when he taught that physical pain is also experienced by the soul. Experience intense emotional pain and you know that your soul aches as much as your body.

Once pain has reached a certain threshold, it expands beyond our physical reactions and affects our muscles, blood flow, tissues and organs. Deep down, we know that we must take the organic path to healing. We must learn ways to give our bodies the rest, relaxation and peace it needs to survive and thrive.

Carolyn Myss, Ph.D., in her groundbreaking book *The Creation of Health* sums up the healing process in this way:

> *"Wanting to heal requires more than the desire not to die. The will to heal is a far deeper commitment to the healing process. It shows the capacity to enter into a journey of complete transformation of oneself, without compromise or limitations.*
>
> *A person in the midst of the crisis of an illness discovers that the disease experience automatically ignites the process of reevaluating all of the parts of one's life. This 'life review' occurs naturally, like a built-in mechanism that nature provides to assist the body/mind /spirit toward returning to inner harmony.*
>
> *The areas of one's life that are contributing to the creation of disease pour into mind during a life review, as if to say 'Look at this memory, look at this resentment, look at this emotional hurt; this is your opportunity to do something about these feelings.' Though this process can be overwhelmingly frightening and painful, it is nonetheless the organic cleansing of one's inner self that must occur in order to heal."*

There are a few words and phrases in Dr. Myss' quote that need highlighting:

Commitment: This word tells us that the journey isn't going to be easy. To make it through this process, it calls for strength, courage and commitment to oneself.

Transformation: This word tells us that change is going to occur. Unfortunately, most people view change as negative. It isn't. Change renews, reignites and reenergizes. We can change the way we see things. In turn, the things we see change.

Without compromise or limitations: This phrase tells us that this healing process promises to open doors to possibilities we doubt exist in our lives. If we are faithful to ourselves and committed to the person we are becoming, the possibilities are unlimited.

Inner harmony: Of all the gifts we receive when we travel this "hero's journey," the greatest joy is the experience of wholeness, oneness and authenticity. The blurred vision of who we are sharply comes into focus.

Organic cleaning: This phrase indicates that what we are about to embark on is natural and normal. It is an organic process originating from a place inside that is real, truthful and healthy.

If we comprehend the concepts behind these words and phrases, we begin to understand that healing is a normal process within the life of any individual. We are wounded and we heal. That is the entire equation. There is no need for fear, compromise or re-wounding. There is only one path and that is to regain the innocence, uniqueness and individuality that our life experiences have stripped from our well-being.

Once we embark on this journey, there will be times when the emotions and thoughts seem anything but natural. It is during these times of confusion, hurt and pain that we need to stay focused on our mission to heal ourselves. The end product – a happier, healthier, more fulfilling life – is worth every minute of feeling uncomfortable.

Sufi mystic Rumi shares these beautiful words on suffering: "Your defects are the ways that glory is manifested. Don't turn your head. Keep looking at the bandaged place. That is where the light enters you."

So, we've now made the decision to heal. Where do we start? Whether we are at-risk for compassion fatigue or actually suffering the symptoms, it is conceivable that we don't have the self awareness necessary to jump into this complex process of inner healing. In order to begin somewhere, it might be helpful to start by examining your roots – your culture, your family of origin, and where you might have developed a perspective of what life is all about. Let me tell you why.

I was born a caregiver. As with all females in my family, I was raised in a culture that values self-sacrifice. Putting others first was promoted and practiced at every turn – home, church, school, and social interactions. I was taught that if I ever came face to face with someone on the sidewalk, I was to step aside and let the other person pass. A large part of my education was spent on perfecting the art of what David Riesman (1948) in his monography, *The Lonely Crowd*, called "other-directedness." In simple terms, this mode of interacting led to the pattern of meeting the needs of others prior to meeting my own needs. The more I focused outward on the needs of others, the more I was encouraged and praised. It's not surprising that I became increasingly hyper-vigilant to the world around me, and increasingly adept at locating lost and suffering souls. Enough so, that I eventually grew to believe that since these interactions were occurring at such an alarming rate, I must have been "chosen" and bestowed with a very sacred "gift." They all needed me; they really needed me.

I married at a young age more than happy to apply my "God-given talents" to fulfill the needs of my husband and eventually our three children. In return, it was my understanding (i.e., my perception) that I would be loved, cared for and provided for. This model had been handed down from generation to generation in my family without scrutiny. It had worked for every female in my family, or so it seemed. I had no good reason to question the program.

Embracing these cultural customs, the path I traveled from childhood to adulthood appeared seamless. As my own children grew, I was afforded the luxury of offering my caregiving "gift" to my community, where I took on the role of professional volunteer. There wasn't an organization in town that didn't have my name on its helping roster. When a crisis occurred in my life (my husband of 18 years up and left in the middle of one cold December night), my caregiving motives eventually came into question.

Ultimately, my compassion fatigue symptoms surfaced with a vengeance. It was then that I realized, after tremendous soul-searching, that being "chosen" and "gifted" carried a very high personal price tag.

In researching compassion fatigue, I came across an interesting article by journalist Joe Rodriguez in his April 9, 2004 San Jose Mercury News column. He wrote about his relatives providing care for his dying mother. It read:

> "My sister and sister-in-law Angelica are devout Mexican-American Catholics who value 'marianisimo' or emulating the Holy Mother. Like too many dutiful Latina daughters, Edelia (his sister) put her life on hold to care for Mama, without enough outside help."

Two points here. First, although Rodriguez and I tell similar stories about the experience of growing up female, in no way is self-sacrifice, other-directedness, or the patterns inherent in *marianisimo* limited to females. In many households, the caregiving torch is passed along to the males in the family. Being born male alone will not protect you from experiencing compassion fatigue. If anything, being born male will make your healing journey a tad bit more difficult. Society places a unique set of expectations on males, and being in touch with your "inner self" certainly is not one of them.

Second point: The purpose of sharing our stories, as I've been doing on these pages, is not to criticize or dissect cultural and religious traditions. Again, compassion fatigue does not play favorites. The purpose of sharing our stories is to kindle a fire in us to bring forth *our* personal narrative. It may not seem so to you right now, but your story contains unimaginable riches even though it may reflect a life laden with loss. Studies show that through storytelling it is possible to expose our emotions and heal our wounds. To take it a step further, storytelling might even allow us to explore the concept of forgiveness and allow that shift to aid in our healing. Nobody wants to hear stories riddled with pain, suffering and loss, but it is imperative to the healing process. The time for tiptoeing around uncomfortable issues has passed.

So, now what? How do we open those psychological doors that have been locked tightly for weeks, months, probably years? The concept and practice of "mindfulness" will help. Since many of us who feel a pull toward caregiving are "other-directed," we have a strong tendency to look outside of ourselves for answers. We might spend countless hours talking to a beloved sister or a football buddy, reading every self-help book on the bestseller list, or even call into a radio station where a favorite celebrity psychologist is espousing a 30-second fix. In the end, no matter how much advice and data we collect from other sources, we must go inward to find what we're looking for. What is the most efficient way to find the answer we seek? Ask ourselves the right questions.

If you are fortunate to live near relatives, there is no better exercise than to play "fly on the wall" when you have a family gathering. Most likely, you'll want to jump right in and act out the role you've been assigned within your family structure. Avoid this. Instead, look and listen. How do your family members interact?

What words do they use to express themselves? Or what words do they withhold in order to NOT express themselves? Place a label on the roles different members play. Is there an antagonist who gets everyone riled up and then steps back? Is there a caregiver who is constantly filling everyone's glass and offering food? Is there a silent member? One who says nothing, but perhaps observes? Is there the family know-it-all? How about a family tease?

The key to locating the authentic self can be found within the interactions of those who helped define the role we play. If our family is scattered all over the country, or even all over the world, the chore becomes more difficult, but not impossible. If you have a family member, maybe an aunt or uncle, or close childhood friend, ask that person some questions. What does he remember about growing up? What does he remember about you? Were you studious? Athletic? The class clown? Did you ever voice your life goals? What profession did you want to pursue? Chances are that person will recollect memories that elude you.

If you haven't anyone to ask, and watching your family in action is not an option, then you must delve into your past alone. It is possible. Begin by recalling memories about your childhood. What was your favorite book? Your favorite fairytale? Who was your favorite character? Favorite game? Favorite television show? Favorite movie? What did you like to do? Think? Write? Draw? Play with your dog, Fido? Dance? There are many clues buried in your memory.

This exercise may sound simplistic and maybe even silly, but it isn't and its value was certainly true in the case of my daughter, Elizabeth. As a young girl with two older brothers whom she adored, she was your consummate "tomboy." She was attracted to science and math, both historically labeled as male-oriented subjects. She was highly competitive and refused any offer that she considered "girlie," such as applying nail polish, wearing jewelry or wearing a dress with lace attached. While I don't want to give credence to stereotypes, it was easy to see that she preferred the more masculine choices and activities of her brothers.

One Christmas her grandmother decided Elizabeth should have at least one doll in her childhood. So she gave her a very lifelike baby doll. Elizabeth, who was only 7 at that time, immediately named the baby doll John Glenn, after the astronaut, which surprised everyone since we had no idea she was even familiar with John Glenn. John went into the toy chest shortly after December 25th and was never seen again.

The point of this story: Many years later in college she received her degree in astronomy and physics, went on to receive her M.F.A. in Science and Natural History Documentary Filmmaking, received a Fellowship at NASA (National Aeronautics and Space Administration) and ended up as the astro-physics producer for NASA Television.

Naming her baby doll John Glenn, which became a family "classic" story held clues to her future and ultimately to her talents and interests.

The same is true for you. For those of us who either suffer from compassion fatigue or are at-risk, our passions in life were probably lost along the way in order to provide care to others. Or perhaps having dreams that define us were never developed due to the fact that our hyper-vigilance took up all of our energy.

It is our passions that sustain us during times of crisis, sadness and loss. Our passions give us hope and a way to work through our grief, ultimately telling us that life is still good. Whether we write, skydive, meditate, cook, paint or do yoga, we need to have that outlet at hand. When most of our day is spent *emptying* ourselves giving care to others, it is these passions that *fill* us up again so we can go out and *empty* ourselves in service to others again

This concept is at the heart of healthy caregiving - empty, fill up, empty, and fill up again.

The difference between unhealthy caregiving that leads to compassion fatigue and healthy caregiving that leads to fulfillment and satisfaction is knowing what it is that renews our emotional, mental, physical and spiritual resources – and fills us up. The great French mathematician Blaise Pascal once stated: *By means of diversion, a man can avoid his own company 24 hours a day.* The amount of time and energy we've diverted our attention to others is most likely in direct proportion to how much or how little we know of ourselves. Too many times our personal resources have been strained beyond repair in hopes of fulfilling the needs of others. This is the reason why introspection is necessary as a starting point. Childhood toys, books and dreams will lead the way to a higher level of your own self-awareness.

Each one of us is a rare blend of genetics, experiences, culture and knowlodgo. In training and dcvclopmcnt, wc call this our "window of perception." Our "reality" creates the eyepiece from which each one of us views the world and everyone and everything in it. This is the lens through which we decide how to cast our vote on Election Day, what car to buy, where to go to school, when to begin or end a relationship, and how to live our lives.

Our window of perception also generates our value system. We live in a world of unlimited choices. Next time you need a pair of tennis shoes, take note of the variety available to you. Not only color, style and cost, but brand and image as well. And that's just shoes – a solid product you can hold in your hand. When we focus on the intangible decisions available to us such as ideas, values, concepts, the field widens and becomes incomprehensible. It is no wonder most of us choose to embrace the tried-and-true value systems of our family of origin, our tribe. It's often just easier than developing an entire life system of our own!

Now think of your window of perception in terms of caregiving. If you hail from a family full of doctors and nurses, chances are that you view caregiving in a positive light. Doctors and nurses hold a place of high esteem in our society, and, therefore, there might be an expectation placed on you to continue the medical lineage. If your tradition is one of high idealism, caregiving might be viewed as an obligation, an inherent debt paid to society. Or perhaps your tradition is one of responsibility and, at an early age, you experienced a system that rewarded putting the needs of others first. Whatever your tradition, these systems hold the capacity to profoundly affect lives generation after generation. For the most part these values, often unspoken, are handed down without benefit of examination. They are purely and simply accepted.

When this happens, life decisions are made from a place of comfort as opposed to a place of choice.

Take some time to peer into your window of perception concerning caregiving and locate those indicators before the seeds of compassion fatigue take root. It is possible to learn to manage compassion fatigue symptoms even before you experience them! Somewhere, buried deeply no doubt, lies the motivator as to why caregiving is "calling" you. Whether you have answered the call through a healthy decision-making process or flipped a coin because you needed some direction, this internal work will be of value to you.

So what exactly is internal work? To begin with, it means stopping, or at least slowing down, to take a look at ourselves in a new light. It means learning to think about what you do and say. It means being mindful of who you are. It means taking an authentic interest in yourself! Unfortunately, talking to oneself has been given a bum rap. But maintaining a healthy ongoing dialogue is the fastest, more sure-fire way to reveal pieces of your inner workings. If we practice this skill of self awareness, we begin to connect the dots which lead to a bigger picture. We then open ourselves to self-illuminating moments, often referred to as Great Aha's! These moments of clarity are the result of time spent on the internal questioning that springs from a need to know, to understand, to comprehend.

Below is a rather entertaining story about an internal dialogue that I experienced several years ago. As trivial as this story may seem, this event both startled and stunned me. The dialogue materialized in my mind instantaneously in front of a bathroom mirror and taught me two very important life lessons. One, humans have the capacity to manifest outside what is going on inside. Two, once a Great Aha! surfaces, there is no turning back. These breakthroughs or insights don't just happen, although it can feel as if they do. After this event occurred, I realized that while the thoughts, feelings and subsequent questions felt instantaneous at the time, the work to get there had taken me months, perhaps even years. I had to be ready to accept the information. Here is what happened:

I was once a shoulder pad lover. Not only did I wear them with every garment of clothing I owned, I kept a stash of different sized pairs in my upper left-hand dresser drawer. Before going out, I stood in front of the mirror to discern if my outfit was balanced with the right sized shoulder pads. If not, I'd call in the replacements and add larger, more substantial ones. One day while standing in front of the bathroom mirror brushing my hair, I stopped abruptly. My eyes filtered down to my oversized shoulders. As if shot from a cannon, a perfectly timed sequence of question ignited the following inner dialogue:

Q. Why in the world am I wearing shoulder pads in my

bathrobe?

A. To make my shoulders larger.

Q. Why?

A. Because I need large shoulders to carry all of my responsibilities. The bigger the shoulder pads, the more I can carry.

Q. Why?

A. Because the world continues to give me more and more responsibility.

Q. Why?

A. Because the world knows I'll take it on.

Q. Why?

A. Because it is expected of me.

Q. Why?

A. Because I have no choice.

Q. Why?

A. Because it is my role. Being the responsible one has always been my role in life. That's who I am.

Q. Why?

A. Because as a child, that is the one place I remember receiving positive feedback and being validated. It made me feel like a good, caring person.

While I was shocked by the revelation that I continued to measure myself by an outdated familial yardstick, I was even more stunned by the fact that I didn't believe I had a choice! How much of this charade I'd been protecting was due to my perception and not based on reality? Once aware that my perceptions were no longer viable and actually causing me pain and distress, I was able to create a shift that propelled me in a better, healthier direction.

Caregiving is an emotional roller coaster ride. The joy that caregiving creates can be tempered with sadness, loss and feelings of despair. This is especially true when compassion fatigue wrestles away emotions, passions and inspiration. With those thoughts in mind, a new paradigm might help. This idea originated with a friend, a psychologist, who teaches her clients this skill on their very first visit. In short she asks, if an idea or question is discussed that causes strong negative or defensive feelings when trying to discern your story, think curious. Instead of allowing your thoughts to stray to that place that elevates your heartbeat, blood flow and anxiety level, focus on being curious. You might even practice asking yourself this simple question: Isn't that curious that it affects me so much?

When we remain curious instead of negative or defensive it allows us room to take in data and process it on a non-personal, non-threatening level. When the behavior becomes curious as opposed to personal, it somehow becomes more palatable. Instead of closing off when we hear something that challenges our emotions and deep-seated beliefs, we can learn to stay open to new possibilities. This, in turn, leaves our brain free to formulate insights concerning outdated modes of thinking, unhealthy habits, and self-defeating behaviors. All of which lurk under the skin; all fodder for compassion fatigue.

This shift will take some time especially if you tend to be other-directed. Look at it this way: You've been very curious about others for a long, long time. Isn't it time to be curious about yourself?

Revealing your roots of compassion fatigue is a process that includes awareness, knowledge, skills, and most important, commitment. And making a long term commitment to create robust inner health is, perhaps, one of life's most difficult concepts. Many of us who suffer believe we have no control over what happens to us. Perhaps we see ourselves as accident-prone, undeserving of good things in our lives, or just plain unlucky. This kind of deep-seated negativism doesn't just appear one day. It has a history that took hold early on. It might have been modeled by caregivers, taught as a family value, or is a result of unhealthy childhood experiences. Any way you look at it, negativity about our abilities leave a disturbing residue on our lives.

Carolyn Myss continues in *The Creation of Health* to share an understanding that entering into the healing process is both frightening and difficult, but ultimately leads to our ability to create good health within our body, mind and spirit. She writes:

> *"In truth, each of our lives contain fears, confusion and pain. In this, we are all identical. It is not necessary to become physically ill to realize we are often controlled by insecurities. The experiences in our lives – our relationships, our careers, our lifestyles – all contain elements of what frightens us. Knowing this provides us with a scope of genuine compassion so that when we are with someone who is ill, including ourselves, we are able to realize that they are in the process of healing much more than just the physical body. Whether illness strikes in our bodies in our individual life environments, it brings to each of us the same challenge – to heal that which we fear about ourselves and about life. And regardless of where and how we encounter our illness, the path of genuine healing will always direct us toward expanding our capacity to take more responsibility for our inner selves and the power of creation that exists within us."*

As Dr. Myss points out, we have tremendous power over what happens to us. We make decisions every day, sometimes unknowingly, that have a profound effect on our lives. While many people revel in making decisions and carefully maneuvering the path their lives take, others are terrified and fearful of having such control. Appearances may deceive. Presenting an image of being in complete control of one's life can be just that, an image. We all know someone who fills that bill. The woman who presents an appearance of having the perfect life, but one day, it all falls apart. We learn that she is filled with regrets, pessimism and anger at herself for the decisions she failed to make. Or the man who looks the part of the sophisticated, highly paid professional, who in the morning newspaper is being indicted for embezzling his company out of millions of dollars.

Years ago, my son Blake was asked to serve as Best Man in a friend's wedding. His friend Greg, an extremely creative and aware individual, made the decision to marry himself. As the editor of the weekly newspaper, Greg decided to wed himself while in the process of writing a feature story on the subject of relationships. We all had a good laugh about Greg's antics with plentiful jokes about the wedding night and honeymoon. But the poignancy of his actions was not lost on any of us. Underlying this humorous event was a profound message: Making a commitment to oneself is about taking personal responsibility and may be the only authentic precursor to making a healthy commitment to another. This bond, this commitment to one's self, is also at the heart of providing healthy care to others.

So what exactly does taking personal responsibility look like? Most likely it would include the ability to make firm, positive choices as to lifestyle, finances, relationships, careers, and even leisure time activities. Certainly it would include respecting and validating others. In today's stressful world, the list would include healthy food choices, no smoking, plenty of exercise, responsible drinking, and at least 7-8 hours of sleep per night. While it isn't easy to attain such high standards every day of every week, at least most of us attempt to meet these goals the best way we can. And if we're fortunate, we had parents or guardians who also made the attempt, which confirmed to us the importance of creating a healthy lifestyle.

But what about those of us who never had healthy modeling from childhood? What about the children whose caregiving adults modeled toxic behaviors such as alcohol or drug dependency, sexual addictions or involvement in abusive relationships? Most likely, we will grow up lacking healthy life coping skills. This inability to deal with life from a healthy perspective leads to chaos, suffering, and unmitigated loss. Ultimately, personal boundaries are blurred, leaving us susceptible to compassion fatigue when placed in the position of caregiver.

Authentic, sustainable healing is a complex process that begins with the decision to live a better life. If a caregiver is living in crisis or chaos, making the decision to heal might be the only road back to mental, physical, and spiritual good health. Taking responsibility for our own well-being demands self awareness, intelligence, knowledge, and time. It's no wonder many of us never make that decision. Taking responsibility for one's self is, plain and simple, a lot of work. Even when we make huge strides, we often find ourselves back to square one.

The root causes of compassion fatigue are usually deeply-seated and are as varied in organic composition as each one of us. The causes listed below give an overview of possibilities. For most of us who suffer from the symptoms, there is one "core" issue that resonates and surfaces routinely. We become what we do repeatedly. That one dominant issue is in the driver's seat and controls when and where the compassion fatigue symptoms surface. Often, avoidance and/or denial are present, allowing the issue to fester as a deeply held hurt.

Because personal stories, backgrounds and perceptions vary from person to person, it is best to look at the causes of compassion fatigue, and then let you, the reader, pinpoint where your truth lies. The following are causes of compassion fatigue followed by definitions that, hopefully, will lead you to a starting place to begin your healing journey.

- PLACING THE NEEDS OF OTHERS BEFORE OUR OWN NEEDS: The majority of our patterns and habits began very early in our lives. We carry those messages in our heads and, without thinking, can often do damage to ourselves. Compassion fatigue is definitely associated with damaged "tapes" that replay over and over again in our minds, which most often hold our hearts captive. If there was dysfunction within our family unit, one family member was designated as the caregiver. This was most likely accomplished in a psychological manner. If you were the family member in charge, you learned from a very early age to place the needs of others before your own needs.

- UNRESOLVED PAST TRAUMA AND PAIN: Dysfunction within the family unit created trauma and pain for everyone involved. We all survive by playing different roles. Some become the peacekeepers; others become the caregivers. While still others choose to just check out and withdraw from the drama. If this is the case within our family of origin, chances are good we've learned to deal with the ill effects by "stuffing" them inside. As a result, the trauma and pain remain unresolved. It is within this unresolved pain and suffering that compassion fatigue takes hold.

- LACK OF HEALTHY PROFESSIONAL AND PERSONAL LIFE COPING SKILLS: If drama, whether constant or intermittent, takes place within our family unit, parents have no time to foster healthy, sustainable life skills in their children. For the most part, the parents are acting out the pain and trauma that they experienced in their own childhood. Family members learn to survive by employing unhealthy patterns and habits such as alcohol, drugs, sex and other addictive behaviors. Low level survival tactics take precedent over applying healthy life coping skills. Eventually, these unhealthy skills translate into unhealthy personal and professional habits.

- LACK OF SELF-AWARENESS THAT LIMITS POTENTIAL GROWTH AND CHANGE: Sadly enough, these limiting patterns continue generation after generation. There is hope, of course, and that hope takes root in awareness. Breaking dysfunctional patterns can and does occur. It only takes one person to acknowledge, accept and go through the pain to get to the other side, which is healthy self-care and personal empowerment.

- GIVING CARE TO OTHERS UNDER STRESS OR BURNOUT: If we don't learn how to effectively take care of ourselves so we have mental, physical, emotional and spiritual reserves, we are going to experience stress and negativity. Burnout is sure to follow.

- LACK OF PERSONAL BOUNDARIES: For the most part, compassion fatigued caregivers have never learned the fine art of saying "no." We labor under the misconception that the best way, sometimes the only way, we receive validation and support is by giving care to others. Since we thrive on validation from others (remember, we're "other-directed"), we can never do enough. And in extreme cases, we suffer a double dose because what we do is never *good* enough. We become like little hamsters running on treadmill wheels, getting nowhere fast.

- INABILITY TO COMMUNICATE NEEDS: In order to experience true happiness and feel in control of our lives, we need to be able to effectively express our needs, desires and dreams. If, throughout our lives, we haven't had anyone at the other end to listen and validate who we are, there is a good chance we have not learned the fine art of communication. With compassion fatigue, our needs are sometimes expressed, but not in a healthy way. They come out as emotional outbursts, usually laced with anger. And directed at anyone who happens to be close by.

- OVERDEVELOPED SENSE OF RESPONSIBILITY: Again, if healthy role modeling was not present during our formative years, we grow without the perspective necessary to moderate our emotions and thoughts. If we were children of divorce, alcoholism, drug or sex addictions, or any other malfunctioning "circle of care," the chances are excellent that we were put in the position of giving care to siblings, our parents and possibly even other relatives. In essence, we were not able to experience a childhood that allowed us the room to dream and explore.

This list of causes may sound dismal to you, but the truth is that once the core cause is recognized, it is quite possible to work through the pain and trauma. Awareness is the first step that leads to the path of recovery and healing, which are always possible. If at any time you deeply doubt your recovery is possible, you might need the assistance of a mental health professional. If so, it may be the best money you've ever spent.

In the beginning, we must uncover our motivation for giving care to others. Is it your true calling? Do you feel you have been chosen or gifted with this special responsibility? On the other hand, does being a caregiver carry a sense of obligation? Overwhelming expectations? Was your choice influenced by someone you admire? A parent? A teacher? Or maybe it just seemed like a good path at this time in your life. Whatever your reason, it is uniquely your own. If you've chosen the path through introspection and insight into who you are and what you have to offer, caregiving can be highly motivational and healthy. If the path has chosen you without due respect to your personality, temperament and talents, caregiving can be highly draining and unhealthy. This road, sadly enough, leads directly to compassion fatigue.

✳

※

CHAPTER FIVE: STANDARDS OF SELF-CARE

If we recognize compassion fatigue symptoms in ourselves, chances are excellent that we've been ignoring our own health needs for a long, long time. We need to change, we want to change and we will change. But sustainable change takes time. The changes we need to employ might include learning new skills and developing new patterns. If we've had financial trouble in the past, we'll have to learn how to budget and manage our financial resources. This might even include looking for a new job that pays us what we're worth. We might decide it's time to lose weight and regain our physical strength. This might include reading books on practical weight management or taking a class on nutrition.

While this new venture is exciting and stimulating to think about, we don't want to overburden ourselves with new practices and processes. Energy levels lag when we suffer the effects of compassion fatigue. The mind might be willing, but the body and emotions are extremely tired due to the limitations we've been experiencing. Building blocks to better health - mind, body and spirit - are just that, building blocks. We have the power to create a stronger, more adaptable foundation by following a prescribed course. The good news is that everything we need to attain authentic, sustainable self-care is within reach.

Healthy self-care can be achieved in two steps: First, we need to truly understand what compassion fatigue is and how it has manifested in our lives. Second, we need to be able to recognize not only what we need to change, but how to start making those changes. Working toward a balanced lifestyle will mean "unlearning" bad habits along the way. Again, we become what we do repeatedly. If we eat poorly and grab fast food on a regular basis, it's going to be difficult to break that habit. If we use alcohol, drugs or food to suppress difficult emotions, it's going to be difficult to overcome those addictions. But just because something is difficult doesn't mean we will fail when we attempt to stop doing what we repeatedly do. It will just take a high level of dedication, knowledge and resiliency to stick to our self-care plan.

For many compassion fatigue sufferers or those at-risk, the concept of self-care is foreign. When we are so busy taking care of others, how can we find the time and energy to care for ourselves? Fortunately, standards of self-care have been created by mental healthcare professionals who understand the needs of the high-functioning, healthy human being. These standards provide the norm, the basics, for achieving a balanced, sustainable lifestyle. Physical, psychological and interpersonal aspects of our lives are included, as well as our spiritual needs. Here is a breakdown of what you need to consider when making plans to treat yourself with kindness and gentleness:

OUR PHYSICAL NEEDS: In order to sustain our physical needs we must learn to integrate the following into our lives:

- Good Nutrition - Providing our bodies with the appropriate foods to promote and ensure good physical health. Monitoring overuse of drugs, alcohol, tobacco and medications.

- Restful sleep and relaxation – Acquiring 7-8 hours of uninterrupted sleep and taking breaks throughout the day to re-energize.

- Regular exercise – Conducting an exercise program that

is tailored to our individual needs, age and temperament.

OUR PSYCHOLOGICAL NEEDS: In order to recognize our psychological needs we must learn to integrate the following into our lives:

- Lifestyle balance – Learning to sustain healthy work hours with healthy recreation time.

- Find our passions – Pinpointing activities and creative outlets that fill us up and re-energize us.

- Stress reduction – Applying mindfulness stress techniques that recognize and honor self-awareness in order to promote change and personal growth.

- Build personal boundaries – Learning to say no when necessary to preserve and respect our limitations.

- Expand life coping resources – Acquiring new skills that promote our well-being such as time-management, effective communication and self assessment tools.

OUR INTERPERSONAL NEEDS: In order to develop our interpersonal needs we must learn to integrate the following into our lives:

- Build a strong support system – Allowing ourselves to experience commitment and responsible friendships that sustain us during difficult times.

- Become involved – Finding a cause that touches our minds and hearts and keeps us attached to the bigger picture.

- Call for help, when necessary – Asking for help is a strength. Knowing our limits helps us to reach out before too much damage has occurred. Have a plan ready when outside assistance is needed.

OUR SPIRITUAL NEEDS: In order to experience a sense of peace, well-being and belonging in our world, we must learn to integrate the following into our lives:

- A source of strength other than ourselves that we can call on for support and guidance.

- A tradition of prayer, worship or meditation that allows us to disengage from the everyday world and transport us to a place of peace and harmony.

- A practice of rituals that have the power to restore calmness, serenity, continuity and hope to our lives.

A tall order, without a doubt! No one could possibly attack all of these areas at one time. It is most likely impossible. The path to authentic, sustainable self-care is a long and winding road. There are times when we take two steps forward and feel energized and triumphant; there are times when we take two steps backwards and feel dazed and confused. We might even be compelled to throw in the towel, so to speak.

But we don't. The rewards are too great and we have an inner resiliency that will carry us through.

So, what is the best way to proceed and meet with enough satisfaction and success to continue? First of all, accept the fact that we must take baby steps. Most of us have spent a lot of years developing unhealthy habits in order to survive. And now we must disassemble all of the dysfunctional patterns that have caused the symptoms of compassion fatigue or put us at-risk.

If only there were a straight and narrow path to wellness, but there isn't. As with anything worthwhile in this life, we must each determine our own course and walk the walk. There are ideas and suggestions that will help, but for the most part, we are each on our own to forge our path. But that is also the exciting part! And always remember, there are unlimited resources out there to aid and guide you. Carve out two hours on your day off from work and spend the time in the library or your favorite bookstore. Many people have passed this way before and have written exceptional books to help you do the same.

Take time to review the areas mentioned above – physical, psychological, interpersonal and spiritual. Does one area jump out at you? Have you wanted to lose 10 lbs and now you're ready? Have you neglected your spirit or wanted to learn more about the practice of meditation? Would you like to expand your communication base and discover some new friendships? Have you been dreaming of taking a painting class or learning to scuba dive?

All of these possibilities are within reach. Set a goal and don't give up until you are satisfied. Then set another goal. By placing one foot in front of the other we learn to move forward and propel ourselves into the realm of good health.

As always, if you feel you need professional help to get you where you want to go, reach out. When the student is ready, the teacher will appear.

The symptoms and causes of compassion fatigue are difficult enough to comprehend without tossing in another factor or two. Unfortunately, it is necessary to throw stress and burnout into the mix. And it is very important to understand the difference between stress, burnout and compassion fatigue. The physical symptoms, emotional chaos and spiritual wasteland that stress and burnout can create make it difficult to tell these three apart from each other. Remember, if any one of these remains untreated for any length of time, compassion fatigue can overarch both stress and burnout, leaving the sufferer literally paralyzed to break free from the quagmire.

Let's start with stress and how it manifests. Below, I've included symptoms that can surface in both our personal and professional lives, as the two are intertwined. If we practice stress-inducing patterns in our personal lives, we most likely carry those same destructive patterns into our professional lives. In order to imagine this concept, think about the children's toy where the whack of the hammer pounds down the mole only to have it pop up in a neighboring hole. There is no keeping that little guy down.

STRESS in CAREGIVING

Stress originates from:

- Inability to say "no."

- A chronic need to "prove" ourselves to others.

- A lack of respect & support from management/colleagues/ patients/clients.

- A lack of clear-cut responsibilities and authority.

- A lack of organizational skills.

- Constantly working against deadlines.

- Involvement in dysfunctional relationships.

- A lack of restful sleep, good nutrition and enjoyable activities.

One more word about stress: Since we are often "other-directed," it is not unusual to listen to others before we listen to ourselves. Friends and family will try to be helpful and might direct you to "get over it" or "don't let it bother you." As well-meaning as they are, their offerings won't help you.

Medical science knows that each one of us suffers the effects of stress in different ways. For some, it might be sleepless nights where our brains won't turn off. For others, it might be a nagging headache that just doesn't seem to go away. This process you are embarking upon is a process of self-discovery. What works for your sister or your friend may not work for you. Listen to that inner voice and follow your instincts. This will begin the dynamic shift that allows you to be in charge of your own authentic, sustainable life.

Get started in this new direction by examining the following areas for stress: your environment (noisy apartment? crowded living quarters?), your health (chronic allergies? lower back pain?), your relationships (disgruntled work colleagues? abusive personal relationship?), and your life (unfulfilling job? problems with children? feelings of loneliness?).

You may not know it yet, but you possess the power of the alchemist – and that is to change base elements into gold. We all do.

Burnout is a psychological term for the experience of long-term exhaustion and diminished interest, especially in one's career.

BURNOUT in CAREGIVING

Burnout originates from:

- Being seriously stressed.

- Being unable to cope.

- Being underappreciated.

- Being overworked.

Compassion fatigue burnout symptoms can lead to a downward spiral in the life of a caregiver. Eventually, negativity and depression can set in. Often with burnout, professional help is needed to aid in the journey back to health.

COMPASSION FATIGUE BURNOUT IN CAREGIVING

Compassion fatigue burnout originates from:

- Over exhaustion/Poor health.

- Overwhelming feelings of hopelessness.

- Overwhelming feelings of helplessness.

- A loss of purpose in both personal and professional life.

- A continuing withdrawal from activities, relationships.

- A lack of energy and low morale.

There are ways to help prevent the downward spiral that can lead to a disruption in our lives. For the most part, caregivers are a serious lot. We are most likely passionate about the work we do and feel ultimately responsible for reaching goals and objectives and creating positive outcomes. In short, we need to lighten up and learn to forgive ourselves when things don't turn out the way we expect. Author G.K. Chesterton reminds us that the reason angels can fly is because they take themselves lightly.

We also need to learn to give ourselves credit for all that we do accomplish. Below are some helpful hints. Remember, practice makes perfect and we are what we do repeatedly.

COPING WITH STRESS AND BURNOUT IN CAREGIVING

- Accept that the situation itself is stressful.

- Share our feelings with a trusted friend, co-worker or family member Acknowledge others who are experiencing the same.

- Enhance our communication skills to lessen feelings of being unheard.

- Initiate positive actions to change our environment.

- Suggest solutions to proper management.

- Care for our personal needs (i.e., good nutrition, hygiene, exercise).

- Take time away from our stressful situations. Allow others to help.

A good way to remember the difference between Stress and Burnout is this:

- Stress is "too much" – too much work, too much pressure, too many expectations.

- Burnout is "not enough" - feelings of depletion, emptiness, apathy, lack of motivation.

As caregivers, we are often stressed and don't know why. Without realizing the effects that life circumstances have on us, we tend to sweep our feelings of frustration, sadness and turmoil under the rug. On the following pages is a Life Stress Test. In the past 12 to 24 months, which of the following major life events have taken place in your life? Mark down the points for each event that you have experienced this year. When you're done looking at the whole list, add up the points for each event and check your score at the bottom.

Life Stress Test

_____ 100 Death of Spouse
_____ 73 Divorce
_____ 65 Marital Separation or from relationship partner
_____ 63 Jail Term
_____ 63 Death of close family member
_____ 53 Personal injury or illness
_____ 50 Marriage
_____ 47 Fired from work
_____ 45 Marital reconciliation
_____ 45 Retirement
_____ 44 Change in family member's health
_____ 40 Pregnancy
_____ 39 Sex difficulties
_____ 39 Addition to family
_____ 39 Business readjustment
_____ 38 Change in financial status
_____ 37 Death of close friend
_____ 36 Change to a different line of work
_____ 35 Change in number of marital arguments
_____ 31 Mortgage or loan over $30,000
_____ 30 Foreclosure of mortgage or loan
_____ 29 Change in work responsibilities
_____ 29 Trouble with in-laws
_____ 28 Outstanding personal achievement
_____ 26 Spouse begins or stops work
_____ 26 Starting or finishing school
_____ 25 Change in living conditions
_____ 24 Revision of personal habits

_____ 23 Trouble with boss
_____ 20 Change in work hours, conditions
_____ 20 Change in residence
_____ 20 Change in schools
_____ 19 Change in church activities
_____ 18 Change in social activities
_____ 17 Mortgage or loan under $20,000
_____ 16 Change in sleeping habits
_____ 15 Change in number of family gatherings
_____ 15 Change in eating habits
_____ 13 Vacation
_____ 12 Christmas season
_____ 11 Minor violations of the law

_____ **Your Total Score**

This scale shows the kind of life pressure that you are facing. Depending on your coping skills or the lack thereof, this scale can predict the likelihood that you will fall victim to a stress related illness. The illness could be mild - frequent tension headaches, acid indigestion, and loss of sleep to very serious illness like ulcers, cancer, migraines and the like.

LIFE STRESS SCORES

0-149: Low susceptibility to stress-related illness.

150-299: Medium susceptibility to stress-related illness.
Learn and practice relaxation and stress management skills and a healthy lifestyle.

300 and over: High susceptibility to stress-related illness.
Daily practice of relaxation skills is very important for your wellness. Take care of it now before a serious illness erupts or an affliction becomes worse.

Permission to reprint the Life Stress Test received from: Dr. Tim Lowenstein, P.O. Box 127, Port Angeles, WA 98362 www.stressmarket.com.

※

CHAPTER SIX: FOR FAMILY CAREGIVERS

Listening to your father tell his World War II stories for the umpteenth time or driving your mother to her monthly cardiologist appointment both are loving, caring services. But when caregiving turns a corner and you find yourself changing your father's diapers or holding your frightened mother's hand as she heads into triple bypass surgery, a deeper understanding of healthy caregiving is necessary.

Compassion fatigue runs rampant in the lives of family caregivers due to emotionally-charged familial ties. Caregivers must take special steps to remain psychologically and physically healthy. Family caregiving is fraught with highs and lows. In a recent study conducted by www.caring.com, 80% of baby boomers (those born between 1946 and 1964) reported that caring for an aging parent puts a strain on their marriage, while 25% said that caregiving played a major role in their divorce. Needless to say, family caregiving can basically destroy your life if not handled with the proper knowledge and coping mechanisms.

Sadly, most family members are tossed into the caregiving storm without warning and without the skills necessary to provide compassionate, healthy care. Mothers are called to care for their terminally-ill children; husbands are ill-equipped to care for their chronically-ill wives; and adult children are burdened with caring for their aging, infirm parents, while raising their own children. Due to the emotional ties inherent in family relationships, caregivers often fail in their attempts to balance their own lives with the high demands of caregiving. More often than not, the lack of coping skills creates a downward spiral and compassion fatigue sets in to extol a high price on the life of the caregiver and the person in his or her care.

I once presented a family caregivers workshop. It was an intimate group of five women who had been placed unexpectedly in the position of primary caregiver of a loved one. The women, of varying ages, displayed a wide range of knowledge concerning the skills and coping mechanisms necessary to providing healthy caregiving. Three of the participants had a fine grasp on personal boundaries, what was acceptable and what wasn't acceptable in their daily processes and procedures. They honored healthy caregiving guidelines, and also had strong boundaries as to the rights of a caregiver. One woman wasn't as knowledgeable, but open to learning how to improve her caregiving skills and avoid the pitfalls of compassion fatigue. But the most memorable of the five was an elderly woman, whom I'll call Mabel. She was caring for her terminally-ill husband. Very frail and fragile as glass, Mabel wept throughout the first hour of the 3-hour workshop.

When facilitating workshops, it is necessary for a presenter to be skilled in lessening the effects of difficult, emotional or negative people. When I realized that nothing I did was helping this overwhelmed woman to catch her breath and open herself to the assistance being offered, I decided the group would actually focus on her situation and learn from her inability to contain her sadness and feelings of loss. Thanks to the kindness and compassion of the other four participants, re-shifting our focus actually worked.

Mabel did not come to the workshop willingly. I asked Mabel what she knew about compassion fatigue and how she had heard about the course. Through her sobs, she told us how her daughter, one of three, had signed her up, paid the fee and drove her to the class. Apparently, she had no say in the matter.

She immediately explained how difficult it was for her to attend. When asked why, she said because she was the sole caregiver to her husband of 60 years and being away from him would certainly prove harmful to his care.

As the hour wore on, the other participants gently asked about her feelings toward caring for her husband and how she was handling all of the tasks necessary to provide the type of care her husband's condition required. Her sobbing grew hardier with each sentence as she struggled to explain herself. She loved him dearly and felt compelled to care for him. No feelings of remorse, guilt or resentment surfaced. Finally, one of the participants asked the question that gave us all of the answers we needed. She asked: Why don't your children help you? When she answered, you could hear a pin drop. She said: Oh, they want to. But no one can care for him the way I care for him.

The seeds of compassion fatigue sprouted out from every word in that sentence. Wrapped up in her need to be the sole caregiver were all of the misperceptions that lead to stress, burnout and compassion fatigue. Mabel suffered from all three. What she didn't realize was that she was single-handedly keeping her daughters from sharing quality, loving time with their father. The dying process is, and always will be, an integral part of the living process. We live, hopefully, every single minute until we die. We share, we love, and we communicate until we no longer have the biological tools to do so – and then the spirit takes over. Allowing her daughters to care for their father would create a loving bond in those last days that will live long after he departs from this world.

If you find yourself as the primary caregiver of a loved one, first take a deep breath. There is help available and S.O.S. is your first line of defense against the ravages of compassion fatigue. By recognizing and practicing authentic, sustainable self-care, compassion fatigue can be avoided or managed. Standards of self-care include 7-8 hours of restful sleep per night, eating nutritious food, engaging in physical exercise and daily creative outlets, and allowing others to assist you. It is also interacting with your loved one on whatever level is appropriate and possible.

Often times, a family caregiver like Mabel falls into the hole of thinking she is the only one who can give the proper attention and care to another family member. Allowing other family members, friends and neighbors to help during this stressful time is both healthy and sustainable. It allows the caregiver time off to re-energize, process complex emotions and give care from a place of abundance as opposed to a place of depletion.

Mabel loved her husband dearly, but was finally able to see that she was neglecting a large portion of his care. And that was to allow each of their beloved daughters to spend quality time alone with their father to bond, say goodbye and create fond memories of their last times together.

Once she was able to see that it was detrimental to withhold these treasures from her husband, she was able to let go of the overburden of responsibility that she carried.

We are living at a very opportune time to learn more about family caregiving. New paradigms are surfacing which allow both the patient and the caregiver to work together toward solutions. In the past, the burden of the care was on the caregiver. But now, it is recognized that the patient/client/customer must also take an active role in his or her care. It is becoming the responsibility of that person to take a more active role in defining his or her care and how it should be administered. Caregiving is becoming a partnership between those who need the care and those in the caregiving professions. This is a positive move toward each of us learning to carry our own burdens and not place them on others. This alone will go far in alleviating compassion fatigue.

There are unlimited resources for family caregivers. The American Red Cross has reached out to family caregivers throughout the years and offers an exceptional module entitled: Caring for the Caregiver (www.redcross.org). The Department of Health and Human Services' National Family Caregiver Support Program offers many good tips at www.aoa.gov/.

While help on the national level is welcome, I highly recommend going local for assistance. Often when we are thrown into the caregiving waters, the fastest, quickest life jacket can be found right around the corner. Recently, I attended a Senior Walk and Fair at a local shopping mall. I was delightfully surprised to find myriad senior services available in my community. Along with medical booths offering free blood pressure testing, there were organizations and associations who work with seniors to locate everything from caregivers to home repair help – all at no cost. Finding people in your neighborhood to help builds community. If you don't know where to start, call City Hall and speak to the receptionist. Tell her what you need and she'll point you in the right direction. If you are Google-friendly, go online and locate resources there. Take a quick trip to your local library and ask the reference librarian. These uncanny helpers are a warehouse of knowledge, especially about community support. One step will lead to the next and in no time, you will have a list of services you will want to explore.

In the meantime, if you have found yourself in an unexpected caregiving situation, use the following means to off-load the stress that could possibly lead to compassion fatigue:

- Accept what has happened and know that you can and will grow and learn from this difficulty.

- Identify little ways to de-stress yourself. Listen to music, breathe deeply, read, prepare favorite meals, pray. If possible, get out and walk.

- Stay in touch with your support system. Call, email or write to those who give you strength.

- Care for yourself. Take a shower or bath to refresh yourself. Nap, if possible. Watch favorite movies or television shows – the ones that make you laugh or give you pleasure. Leave the detective and crime shows for another time.

- Bring in your pets. If you are an animal lover, allow your pet to give you comfort.

- Plan something for future enjoyment. Have something as simple as a movie or lunch date with a friend to look forward to. While you must stay highly-focused on the present in order to fulfill the needs of your loved one, it never hurts to embrace the future.

A word about pets: If an elderly person in your life is caring for an aging or ill family pet, the process can be devastating and create compassion fatigue. To many people, especially the elderly and those living alone, a pet can provide unconditional love and support. The decision to euthanize Fido is often traumatizing and painful. Provide healthy caregiving to your loved ones by honoring the stages of grief. This goes for the children in your care, as well. Grief comes in all sizes and shapes. Listen, validate feelings and, ultimately, help your loved one select and welcome a new pet, when and if the time is right.

❋

CHAPTER SEVEN: TO THOSE ENTERING THE HELPING PROFESSIONS

Every year, colleges, universities and trade schools churn out bright-eyed, idealistic students of all ages eager to make a mark on the caregiving profession of choice. For whatever reason, they answered a calling and found themselves traveling the caregiving path. Instead of striving to become account executives, CEOs or CFOs, they want to make a difference in the world through service to humanity. And, in fact, many will accomplish their noble goal without anything more than tired bones at the end of the day. But not everyone entering a caregiving profession will be so fortunate. It is now common knowledge that compassion fatigue can cause a form of disillusionment that undermines any good about the choice of profession.

Understanding the causes and consequences of this stress syndrome *before* entering a caregiving profession can be, literally, a lifesaver. Learning to help without harm to yourself and others is a long, slow process. But the symptoms, when left unattended, can rob you of the healthy empathy you need to offer compassionate care to your patients, clients, customers, and very often in caregiving environments, your colleagues. Worse than that, the harmful behaviors stemming from the stress will render you incapable of acknowledging your own achievements – those self-esteem building successes that are crucial to continuing the caregiving work that we value and is so badly needed in our world.

The goal of this chapter is to help you, the aspiring caregiver, to better understand compassion fatigue, who it affects, why, and what can be done to alleviate the energy-sapping symptoms that keep us locked in battle with ourselves.

You might already sense that you or someone you know is suffering from compassion fatigue. It appears that caregiving professions attract those who are most vulnerable - those who are caring, loving, giving, unselfish, inspiring, joyous, empathic people. These same people make the best helpers. So there is no need for panic: You are not destined to a life of pain and suffering. Past events and experiences in your life might have set you up as a prime candidate.

It has been suggested that those of us affected by compassion fatigue hail from a tradition of "other-directed" caregiving. Simply put, we were taught at an early age to care for the needs of others before caring for our own needs. With the proper information and support, it is possible to embark on a journey of self-discovery that will heal the pain and trauma that can currently serve as obstacles to healthy self-care and success in your profession.

As you progress through these pages, it is important that you take the time to think about your choices and, in fact, make sure they are choices and not the expectations of others. You might be called upon to do some very difficult inner work. This could mean revisiting your family of origin where patterns formed early on and now nourish the seeds of compassion fatigue. It might mean changing behaviors that lie at the heart of your comfort zone. It might even mean re-examining your motives for choosing a caregiving profession.

Doug Fakkema is a trainer and consultant who conducts humane euthanasia workshops around the country and in Mexico. He worked as an animal shelter director for 19 years and knows the business inside and out. During the many years of shelter work, Fakkema recognized a set of phases that new employees experienced. He refers to them as the Four Phases of Career Evolution. While he specializes in animal welfare work and he makes references to sheltering, it will quickly become obvious that his explanations can cover any caregiving profession. Below are the four phases:

Phase One

> Red hot and raring to go, we are out to change the world. We are high on life. We know that we can make a difference, that our efforts on behalf of animals will ease their plight. We work what seem like 25-hour days, yet we are energized. Our enthusiasm overflows; our capacity for challenges is limitless. We eat, sleep, and live in the cause for animals. Our friends don't understand our obsession and turn away or just fade away, and we let them, for we meet new ones. Some of us, though, don't make new friends; we're too busy working for animals.

> Some of us become loners with only our canine or feline companions to keep us from total isolation, but we're content because we have a cause. In our zeal, we tend to affix simple solutions to complex problems—every animal should be sterilized or no animal should be euthanized. We're often late because we try to rescue animals from highways and streets. We think we understand the problem, and we know we can fix it if only people would get out of our way.

Phase Two

> Our Phase One enthusiasm has turned sour; the bubble bursts and we crash and burn. We see the same people coming into the shelter with yet another litter—they haven't heard our message. We continue to euthanize;

there seems no end to it. Even our friends—those we still have left—don't understand us. We can't seem to reach anyone.

Animals are still abused and neglected; their plight seems unchanged despite all our efforts. We've lost the boundless energy that characterizes Phase One. We no longer wish to talk about work, don't even want to admit where we work. We're tired all the time. We go home from work, lock the doors, turn out the lights, turn off the answering machine, and close the window blinds. We're too exhausted to cook so we scarf fast food, pizza, potato chips, and chocolate.

Some of us buy useless things we can't afford. Some of us turn to alcohol, for it takes away our feelings of hopelessness. We ignore our families, and even our pets get less attention than we know is right. We seem powerless to affect any of the changes that drove us to such ecstasy of dedication in Phase One. We have become horrified by the work we have to do. Even our dreams are filled with the horror. Every animal we take in and every animal we euthanize is yet another nail in our coffin of defeat. Somehow we're to blame for all the failure, and it's destroying us. Raise the shields, Scotty—the Klingons are on our tail!

Our shield gets thicker and thicker. It blocks the pain and sadness and makes our life somehow tolerable. We continue because every now and then we get a spark of Phase One energy.

Phase Three

Our Phase Two depression has turned outward and we're mad as hell. Hopelessness turns to rage. We begin to hate people, any people and all people unless, like our coworkers, they dedicate their lives to animals the way we do. We even hate our coworkers if they dare to question us—especially about euthanasia. It occurs to us: Let's euthanize the owners, not the pets. Let's take everyone who abuses an animal or even surrenders an animal and euthanize them instead.

Our rage expands to our out-of-work life. That guy in front of us on the highway, the one who's in our way, let's euthanize him, too. We rage at politicians, television, newspapers, our family. Everyone is a target for our anger, scorn, and derision. We have lost our perspective and effectiveness.

We're unable to connect with life. Even the animals we come in contact with seem somehow distant and unreal. Anger is the only bridge to our humanness. It's the only thing that penetrates our shield.

Phase Four

I know I've been in all these phases during my 30 years in animal protection, and Phase Four is by far the best place to be. Some people get frozen in Phase One (the zealots), or Two (the zombies), or Three (the misanthropes). Some shift back and forth between Two and Three and even between Four and Three or Four and Two. Many leave animal work during Phase Two or Three, never to return. Some seem to move rapidly to Phase Four, while for others it takes years and years. Some never get a sense of peace to go along with our purpose; they work their entire lives in the frantic pink cloud of Phase One, or they remain perpetually depressed or angry.

Over time, though, the depression of Phase Two and the anger of Phase Three can become replaced with a new determination and understanding of what our mission really is. This is Phase Four—big picture time. We realize that we have been effective locally—and in some cases, regionally and even nationally. So we haven't solved the problem (who could?), but we have made a difference for dozens, even hundreds and sometimes thousands of animals. We have changed the way others around us view animals. We begin to see our proper place in our own community, and we begin to see that we are most effective when we balance our work and out-of-work lives. We realize that work is not our whole world and that if we pay attention to our personal lives, we can be more effective at work. We understand that some days we work 14 hours and some days we knock it off after only 8. We take vacations and we enjoy our weekends. We come back refreshed and ready to take on daily challenges. We see that all people are not bad. We understand that ignorance is natural and in most cases curable. Yes, there are truly awful people who abuse and neglect animals, but they are a minority. We don't hate them.

When we find them we do all we can to stop them from hurting animals. We recognize that the solutions are just as complex as the problems, and we bring a multitude of tools to solve those problems. We use the tools in any way we can, and we begin to see results—one small step at a time. We reconnect with the animals. Our shields come down. We understand that sadness and pain are a part of our job. We stop stuffing our feelings with drugs, food, or isolation. We begin to understand that our feelings of anger, depression, and sadness are best dealt with if we recognize them and allow them to wash over and past us. We recognize our incredible potential to help animals. We are changing the world.

Fakkema's last phase runs parallel to what author Henry James once wrote about the human condition:

"Sorrow comes in great waves,

but it rolls over us,

and though it may almost smother us, it leaves us

And we know that if it is strong,

we are stronger, inasmuch as it passes and we remain."

Is it possible to avoid these explosive situations as neophytes to the workplace? Quite possibly. As your knowledge and self-awareness grow, so will your ability to make good, solid decisions concerning employment. The fact is that some organizations are simply better to work for than others. Learning to recognize the difference will save you not only time and energy, but will also help you to avoid pitfalls that lead to disillusionment, which can be detrimental to your health and your future success in your career. Hiring into an organization where upper management displays an awareness of compassion fatigue and provides training and support, you will fare much better than if you end up in a place where the Emperor has no clothes and is riding that huge elephant around the room!

Dysfunctional, for lack of another word, workplaces look different to outsiders. The survivors, those who somehow endure such places, have learned to adjust because they may have few other options or they may be part of the reason why it is dysfunctional. There are some tools by which to measure possibilities and recognize "red flags." Bringing compassion fatigue knowledge to your interviews can help in identifying potential hot spots. Ultimately, the decision will be yours as to whether you want to sign on at a particular organization or continue your job search. Be aware that you may feel a compulsion or strong urge to "fix" the organization. Under no circumstances, no matter how talented, intelligent, skilled or committed you may be, you cannot "fix" the organization. The issues causing the dysfunction run deep and, in the end, you will come out wounded and disillusioned. And that is an awful way to begin your caregiving marathon and career.

So, let's look at some of the nuts and bolts of assessing an organization, business or company.

You've completed your area of study and are eager to enter the world of service. None of us would attempt to run a 26-mile marathon without a training program. The same is true in the employment race. Begin by combing the classifieds daily, using both print and Internet sources. Network, if you've already made contact with the type of place you'd like to spend your time. Leave your resume with a favorite instructor or professor. Your mentors and teachers often serve as the link to your future. Share your resume with family and friends. You never know where that job will come from.

It is a very exciting time, but you may feel deep anxiety too. You might be asking yourself the following questions:

Is it possible to find a job I really want? Will I have to relocate? Will I have to leave my family and friends? How much will I get paid? Will my check cover my rent and car payment? Will I have to continue living at home with my parents? What if I don't like my boss? Will I have to work nights, or worse yet, weekends?

These questions are normal and perfectly valid. The transition from student to working professional is fraught with change, decision making and unexpected challenges. As a student, you've probably been able to control your schedule to some degree. You've received assignments in January that weren't due until March, allowing you the freedom to manage the project according to your own timeframe. Even if you have been attending school full time and working part time, you've managed to manipulate your days and nights to include both study and social time.

All of that will shift when you officially enter the working world. Suddenly, your time will be full of assignments and tasks with deadlines set by someone else. While your performance in the classroom only impacted your grade, your performance at work will impact your boss, your co-workers, your customers or clients, and, ultimately the survival of the organization.

By the time you complete your education, chances are good that you have student loans, credit card debt and other financial worries. You are probably looking to break free from parental authority and create your new life as an independent person. All of these reasons and many more could make you eager to jump on the first job offer that comes your way. But don't. Take your time. This is arguably the most important decision you will make at this point in your life.

Job satisfaction surveys show that most adults require the minimum from their workplace: A safe environment, an outlet for creativity, positive interactions and reinforcement, and high on the list of most caregivers, a sense of purpose. A decent salary is always welcome as well! Unfortunately, the way the American economy is structured in the 21st century, that is to say it's all about profit, employers are asking for more and giving less. Competition for good jobs is fierce, putting employers in the power seat. This is especially true in non-profit organizations where the majority of caregiving jobs live. One quick look at the classified job ads and you will see that the workplace is crying out for development directors. Non-profits are all battling for the same grant money and potential donors. This is the environment where many of you reading this book might end up.

It is a sobering fact that much of our life is spent at work. So before you begin interviewing, take time to assess your physical, professional and emotional needs. Physical needs tend to be very obvious. If you are an active person who is energized by being outdoors and performing a variety of tasks, do not apply for a grant-writing position even if it's with an organization that you believe in. Long hours spent at the computer and doing research will make you want to tear your hair out. Professionally, find a position that showcases your strengths and skills. If you are the world's greatest listener, don't settle for a position as administrative assistant to the CEO. Put your talents to work as an intern social worker or psychologist. Make sure you understand your career path. You won't get to where you're going if you take the wrong turn.

Assessing your emotional needs is far more complex. Chances are the reason you have chosen a caregiving profession is simply because you have feelings attached to the work. Animal welfare workers end up in animal shelters because they love animals. Child abuse counselors end up working with abused children and their families because they feel strongly about ending child abuse. Make sure your employment decisions are based solely on the organization's mission matching up with your personal mission. If you don't have a personal mission, create one. Success is based on how well employees, volunteers and board of directors use the organization's mission statement as their guiding light. Best to know up front that neither your boss nor the guy in the next cubicle is there to meet your needs. Only you can meet all of your needs. Figure out what those needs are and determine the best places to fulfill them.

Take time to write a personal mission statement that embraces your hopes and dreams. It could read something like this: It is my mission to secure employment where my talents and gifts are valued and respected and I am paid what I feel I am worth.

Use this statement as a guideline to assess whether or not a workplace can offer you the right stuff. If not, look elsewhere. Positive first work experiences reinforce our commitment to caregiving and provide a strong foundation for our future personal and professional growth. Many first-time caregivers have gone out into the world to a job that was unsuitable and ended up leaving their profession. You've put too much time, effort and money into your schooling to allow that to happen.

Interviewing is a two-way street. Employers are looking for someone to add value to their organization; you are looking for a job that meets your financial, professional, and emotional needs. Even though you may feel stressed, nervous, and discouraged at times, it is important to remember that you hold power, too. In order to get the input that is critical in making a good strong career choice, you will need to ask the right questions. And then listen intently to the answers. If your interviewer makes any off-hand comments, pay attention. A red flag is waving if an interviewer makes cynical, inappropriate, or negative references to management, staff, customers, or volunteers. Organizational compassion fatigue may be under construction there. Formulate your questions carefully to get the answers you need. Use an interviewing plan as a roadmap to steer the process.

Contrary to what most people believe, your relationship with your supervisor is the most important one you will have at work. Sure, it's great fun to have colleagues with whom you share a sandwich at lunch or a movie after work. But it is your supervisor who decides whether you stay or go. Good supervisors are visible, knowledgeable, and supportive. I've worked with a number of supervisors who were so overwhelmed by compassion fatigue that they simply retreated. While physically present on the job, they were professionally and emotionally inaccessible to both colleagues and customers. A manager who practices those behaviors is not going to be able to give you what you need to prosper in your job, which is good mentoring, thoughtful responses, and the tools you require to get your job done. When interviewing, remember to ask questions pertaining to the style of management followed in the organization. Once you have your answers, trust your intuition and choose wisely.

You may be surprised to encounter some negative feedback if you take your time in seeking just the right job. And more so if you actually reject a job offer that doesn't meet your expectations. Often this feedback originates with well-meaning family and friends. Sometimes our loved ones project their own perception of what they believe is best for us – a stable job, a steady income, a position close to home, a comprehensive insurance plan. As difficult as it might be, you must stand your ground. Only you know what's best for you. As a manger, I've conducted countless job interviews in both corporate and non-profit sectors. The most impressive candidates, and those who usually get the job, are those who communicate a healthy confidence in their abilities. They convey an awareness of the need for something in return other than just a paycheck. They are looking for respect, validation, and appropriate payment for work well done.

There is a special nature attached to caregiving jobs. Karen W. Saakvitne, Ph.D. and Laurie Pearlman, Ph.D. discuss it in their laudable book *Transforming the Pain: A Workbook on Vicarious Traumatization.* They write: As researchers and scholars, we understand that it is impossible to hear and bear witness to trauma survivors' experiences and remain unchanged.

When we make a conscious decision to put our time, energy, and talents into one place, *we* change that place. In turn, that place changes *us*. Speaking from my own experiences, that change can be uplifting and life-affirming, or it can be devastating and degrading. Due to the emotional and physical stress involved with giving care to others, when a caregiving job goes sour, your life can be turned upside down. The healing process that follows the fall-out can take months, maybe even years. There is often betrayal, retaliation, and revenge involved due to the emotional nature of the work. If an employee finds herself pitted against management for whatever reason, the very clients or customers you signed on to nurture often end up victimized by the negativity surrounding the situation. The pain involved can become overwhelming and chronic if not treated professionally.

You now have awareness and hopefully helpful information that you need to define and label compassion fatigue both in the individual and the workplace. This will help you choose your place of employment with eyes-wide-open. A positive start in your caregiving profession can begin to build a foundation of healthy, purposeful service to others. This foundation can strengthen and propel you into the years ahead where success and fulfillment will keep you passionate about the work you do. And more important, these healthy self-awareness and self-care principles will not only offer you support while running the race, but also carry you to the finish line.

☀

CHAPTER EIGHT: WHEN THE WORKPLACE SUFFERS

While working at the animal shelter, I trained and mentored at least 25 entry level caregivers. Consistently, over the course of time, I witnessed the four phases of caregiving being played out. And not one had a positive ending. I watched happiness nosedive into sadness; courage overcome by fear; and resolve mutate into apathy. Not one employee was spared. As a trainer, I was pulled into every drama. When an employee had been "written up" a number of times, it was my job to schedule a one-on-one training to weed out the root of the misconduct. During those sessions, employees expressed so much negativity and despair about the workplace that I began to wonder what else was going on. I had done my part in training the employees the best way possible, and other managers had done the same in their areas of expertise. It wasn't until I compared the working environments of these fledgling caregivers to those of my own three adult children that I found my answer.

When it came time for my two sons and my daughter to choose a profession, each one chose from the heart – theater, marine biology, and science and natural history documentary filmmaking. After college, when entering the workplace, each experienced aspects of the four phase marathon as they transitioned from student to professional, but without the despair or discouragement that I witnessed in the young shelter caregivers. There were frustrations and mistakes made, of course, but for the most part my children were energized and strengthened throughout the process, while the shelter employees were demoralized and weakened.

It occurred to me that something else was at the heart of the problem. The shelter caregivers never made it to the finish line. Could it be that the organization itself contributed to the employee's inability to complete the race and ultimately add to the disillusionment of its workforce? It was then that I realized that the symptoms of compassion fatigue as noted in Chapter One not only held the power to affect the individual, but the organization as well. How could they not? The employees *are* the organization!

When compassion fatigue among employees hits critical mass, the organization itself suffers.

I witnessed this not only in animal welfare, but also in my job working with children with life-threatening illnesses, working in an elder care facility, and also a six-hospital healthcare system.

The organizational symptoms serve to magnify and escalate the individual symptoms, thus creating a vicious compassion fatigue cycle. Chronic absenteeism, high turnover rates, spiraling Worker's Compensation claims and costs are just a few of the symptoms that seep into every corner of the afflicted workplace. When left unaided, stress levels rise. Employees, particularly the line staff and middle management, feel helpless, then hopeless. Resentment, hostility and blame surface. These behaviors, sparked by the burgeoning symptoms of individual compassion fatigue, induce rampant rumors, gossip, and unhealthy competition between co-workers.

I once entered the animal shelter break room only to overhear two employees talking. An older man, a facilities manager who had been on the job for 15 years, and a younger man, a kennel manager who had joined the staff only 3 months prior, were arguing with their claims accelerating at a rapid rate. The interaction sounded something like this:

"I put in at least 60 hours last week," the facilities manager stated with great pride.

"Well that's nothing," the kennel manager boasted. "I put in at least 70 hours."

"Hey, I've been here longer than you and I've seen my share of 80 hour weeks," the older manager shot back.

The competition lasted about five minutes with each employee displaying his expertise in one-upmanship. Finally, a beeping pager signaled the end of the contest and nudged the younger man back into the kennels. As an onlooker, I was saddened to watch two good people competing for the winning spot as the #1 self-abuser.

In my experience, the non-profit environment plays host to these symptoms more often than its counterpart, the for-profit corporation. Although I have heard other professionals disagree. For the most part though, the day-to-day challenges of running a non-profit are exacerbated by low wages, lack of space, lack of funding, high management turnover, and constantly shifting priorities. Because of the enormity of the obstacles they face, denial is often the path of least resistance. It isn't unusual to find an "elephant in the room" when working for a non-profit. Until that enormous gray guy sitting in their midst is acknowledged, management cannot move forward with the healing necessary for a healthy work environment. Cartoon character Charlie Brown of *Peanuts* fame, once proclaimed: There is no problem so large that it can't be run away from. But running away from the pachyderm known as compassion fatigue only serves to create additional obstacles.

Often, these obstacles are created at the top and filter down. It has been my experience that a non-profit executive director who has been in her job for ten years or longer is a prime target for burn-out and compassion fatigue. It is safe to say, that after so many years, a grasp on the mission of the organization, which is always in the best interest of the disenfranchised, is lost. The inability to handle all of the loss and pain she has witnessed turns to despair, negativity and denial. In turn, the next level of management, usually the directors, receive the brunt of her stress, which manifests as abuse and harassment. When directors experience the same behaviors, they pass them along to middle management. And so on down the line until, finally, the compassion fatigue symptoms affect the client. When this occurs, all chances of healing, both mentally and physically, are in jeopardy.

Heart-driven people are attracted to non-profits like dieters are attracted to cream puffs. Finding Fido a good home or bringing Meals on Wheels to homebound seniors is what we serious caregivers crave in this world. It is our heart's mission – our passion – that propels us out of bed in the morning eager to face yet another day of giving care to the abused, pained and suffering. But when passion rules both head and heart, watch out. The unbridled passion of caregivers is arguably at the core of organizational compassion fatigue. The same emotions that jolt us out of bed can also steer us right into a minefield where our hopes and dreams get blown to Jupiter and back, leaving us with shards of disillusionment to contend with.

At this time, there is much work to be done in researching and collecting data concerning organizational compassion fatigue. Members of the Compassion Fatigue Awareness Project© Forum have written their impressions of their workplaces – and many times, the symptoms of organizational compassion fatigue are present. The good news is that caregivers from all professions are now becoming aware of this possibility and understand the toll it can take on staff, clients, customers, and volunteers, along with the structure and success of the organization itself.

We all have reason to believe that the future holds only good, solid information on how we can either combat compassion fatigue before it takes hold or lessen its effects in the workplace through diligent training and development workshops.

✴

✳

CHAPTER NINE: TO WEEP FOR A STRANGER

Caregiving paradigms are changing rapidly in America as well as the rest of the world. In order to survive the trauma and tensions that are now inherent in our society, caregivers must learn new lines of defense in order to survive. Caring isn't nearly enough. Now, we must arm ourselves with knowledge and coping skills while building new bridges to create authentic, sustainable self-care practices into our busy lives. We must be willing to reflect inward while maintaining a calm and cool demeanor outward. This recipe gives us the best shot at developing into compassionate caregivers.

An awareness of compassion fatigue is our first defense against acquiring its debilitating symptoms. We are fortunate to have so much information to guide us in our caregiving mission. Years ago, the pain and suffering caregivers experienced had no label, no data, and no name. Today, we take on our tasks with our hearts and minds open to the risks. We know compassion fatigue is real and we are at risk

While there are unlimited areas of study we can pursue as far as caregiving, one of the most growth-oriented and secure professions we can head into is healthcare. As the Baby Boomers age, we are going to be challenged to provide more quality, compassionate care than ever before. The numbers are staggering. Currently, it is estimated by the American Red Cross that more than 22 million families are caring for a loved one at home. This is a thick slice of the caregiver pie. Add caregivers in hospitals, assisted living facilities, hospices, mental institutions, child advocacy, welfare and social workers and the list becomes endless.

As science advances in areas such as organ and tissue donation, stem cell research and transplants, caregivers in a number of arenas such as medicine and healthcare, will be touched by daunting decisions, dilemmas and ethical questions. A need for good, strong verbal and communication skills, as well as negotiation and mediation talents will be called upon. Caregiving boundaries will continue to expand and include husbands, wives, partners, children and other relationships. As we stretch our resources, we will be more at-risk for compassion fatigue than ever before. Defining our personal boundaries will become mandatory as we incorporate the model of caring for the whole person – mind, body, and spirit.

The perimeters of caregiving are going to continue to expand to include innovative safety techniques, legal knowledge, a broader understanding of advanced caregiving directives, traumatology training and end-of-life issues. Caregivers will need to be well-versed in the use of intricate medical equipment, administration of medications and medical record technology. More interaction with family members will include the need for grief counseling and even financial knowledge to help people navigate the ever-complex health care system.

We, the caregivers, will be called on to aid and support our clients and patients in ways we can't even comprehend yet. Life will become a balancing act of the highest order. Our health and well-being will be put to the test. Perhaps there will even be times when our own spirits will be broken. Do we have the resources in place to rejuvenate ourselves? Are we capable of keeping up with the technological advances that add more pressure and stress to our jobs? Do we possess the skills to balance our relationships, both professional and personal? With technology allowing us to be on call 24/7, achieving balance is nothing less than a high wire tightrope walk. On one side, we can gently release our work and all of its implications at the end of the day and go to our loved ones, our hobbies, and our nurturing environments that sustain us. On the other side, we can plunge off the tightrope and find ourselves in the downward spiral known as compassion fatigue.

It is only within the past decade that an understanding of compassion fatigue - its symptoms and its harmful affects - has even surfaced. It has mistakenly been labeled depression, burnout or apathy. We now know that compassion fatigue is a secondary traumatic stress syndrome, attacking caregivers of all ages and professions. Now that the term *compassion fatigue* has hit the "tipping" point, and the concept has become mainstream, you will hear about it and recognize it in the work you do.

Hopefully, the words and thoughts that appear on the previous pages have added to your knowledge, intelligence and resiliency. You can now define compassion fatigue, recognize its symptoms, and understand its causes. You have taken steps to wrestle with your own demons that keep you locked in battle with your emotions and actions. It now makes sense to you that abusing yourself in whatever way is no longer an option. And that you must stand up for yourself even at a time when no one else will.

Keep this book handy. You may want to make reference to it in the future. I highly suggest that you re-take Dr. Beth Hudnall-Stamm's ProQOL R-IV Self-Test regularly as you proceed along your path of healing. It was this Self-Test that first taught me that I was suffering from compassion fatigue and it was this Self-Test taken years later that reassured me that I had information to share. As my scores dropped dramatically, it became crystal clear that it was my newly-engaged practices of self-care that were not only working, but changing my life for the better every step of the way.

You have taken some of those steps yourself. While reading this book, you have experienced pit stops along the way to examine your motives and desires. It is now your duty to take what you've learned and experiment with it. Find out what works best for you. We are each on a different, very unique path to finding our heart's desire and living the life we dream about.

If I were to sum up the heart of this work for you, I would say it is imperative to get to know yourself, know your limits, learn to create personal boundaries that allow you to re-energize and re-kindle your passion for caregiving. And probably most important, believe that compassion fatigue is real. It isn't something that happens to someone else, it can happen to you.

Within the past couple of years, author Kurt Vonnegut died at age 81. I always enjoyed reading his works, but it wasn't until I read his obituary that I realized his level of decency. A caregiver, if you will. The title character in his 1965 novel, *God Bless You, Mr. Rosewater*, summed up Mr. Vonnegut's philosophy in the following way:

> *"Hello, babies. Welcome to Earth. It's hot in the summer and cold in the winter. It's round and wet and crowded. At the outside, babies, you've got about a hundred years here. There's only one rule that I know of, babies — 'God damn it, you've got to be kind.'"*

When all is said and done, healthy, sustainable caregiving is about kindness. Not only kindness to those we serve, but kindness to ourselves. It's about realizing that as caregivers we do the best we can. If we hold the hand of a dying woman and provide her comfort or save one kitten from being euthanized, or counsel one suicidal teenager to understand that she has a whole, wonderful life ahead of her, we have succeeded.

So pat yourself on the back. You're holding steady on your path to wellness. You're poised to become the best caregiver you can be. Your reward is a lifelong love affair with providing kind, compassionate care to others, but most importantly, to yourself.

Yes, we are called upon to weep for a stranger. It is the caring, loving, human thing to do. But we are not called to weep for a stranger at the expense of our own health and well-being. Recognizing and managing compassion fatigue allows us to do both. We are called to walk the path alongside those who are suffering or are in pain; we are not asked to walk their path for them. Their experience of pain and suffering is complex and entwined in their life choices, decisions and experiences. No matter how hard we may try, we cannot truly embrace *their* journey. We can only embrace *our* journey.

In closing, I would like to share with you my favorite story that exemplifies this concept:

Author and lecturer Leo Buscalgia was once asked to judge a contest. The purpose of the contest was to find the most caring child. The winner was a 4-year old boy whose next door neighbor was an elderly gentleman who had recently lost his wife. Upon seeing the man cry, the little boy climbed onto his lap, and just sat there. When his mother asked him what he said to the neighbor, the little boy answered: Nothing, I just helped him cry.

❊

REFERENCES

Hansen, Michael, *"Battling Compassion Fatigue: The Pitfalls and Promise of Modern Altruism,"* ConsciousChoice, Dragonfly Media, December 2001.

Carroll, Lewis, *Alice's Adventures in Wonderland & Through the Looking Glass.* New York: The New American Library of World Literature, Inc., 1960.

Schweitzer, Albert, *Out of My Life and Thought.* Baltimore & London: The Johns Hopkins University Press, 1998.

Sheehy, Gail, *"So Much Good Happened Here,"* PARADE Magazine, Parade Publications, July 21, 2002.

Mandel, Debra, PhD., *Healing the Sensitive Heart: How to stop getting hurt, build your inner strength, and find the Love you deserve.* Avon, MA: Adams Media Corporation, 2003.

Sharon Salzberg, *Loving-Kindness: The Revolutionary Art of Happiness.* Shambahla Classics, Boston, MA, 2002.

Sebold, Alice, *Lucky: A Memoir.* Back Bay Books, Hachette Book Group: Boston, MA, 2002.

Waterston, Ellen, *Then There Was No Mountain: A Parallel Odyssey of a Mother and Daughter Through Addiction.* Lanham, MD: Taylor Trade Publishing, 2003.

Scarf, Maggie, *Secrets, Lies and Betrayal: How the Body Holds the Secrets of a Life and How to Unlock Them.* Ballantine Books, Random House: New York, 2005.

Harbolt, Tami L., *Bridging the Bond: The Cultural Construction of the Shelter Pet.* West Lafayette. Indiana: Purdue University Press, 2003.

Saakvitne, Karen W. and Laurie Anne Pearlman, *Tranforming the Pain: A Workbook on Vicarious Traumatization.* New York: W.W. Norton & Company, 1996.

Glasgow, Ellen, *The Woman Within*, Charlottesville, Virginia: University of Virginia Press, 1994.

Housden, Roger, *Ten Poems to Change Your Life*. New York: Harmony Books, Crown Publishing Group, 2001.

Myss, Carolyn, Ph.D., and C. Norman Shealy, M.D., PhD., *The Creation of Health: The Emotional, Psychological, and Spiritual Responses That Promote Health and Healing.* New York: Three Rivers Press, Crown Publishers, Inc., 1993.

Reisman, D. (with Glazer, N and Denny, R,). *The Lonely Crowd: A Study of the Changing American Character*. New Haven: Yale University Press, 1948.

Vonnegut, Kurt, *God Bless You, Mr. Rosewater.* New York: Dial Press, Random House, 1998.

❀

OTHER TITLES FROM THE COMPASSION FATIGUE AWARENESS PROJECT©

Training Workbooks

- *Healthy Caregiving: A Guide to Recognizing and Managing Compassion Fatigue*

  Presenter's Guide Level 1

  (to order: https://www.createspace.com/3363699)

- *Healthy Caregiving: A Guide to Recognizing and Managing Compassion Fatigue*

  Student Guide Level 1

  (to order: https://www.createspace.com/3363698)

Training Materials

- The Caregiver's Bills of Rights

- The Eight Laws Governing Healthy Caregiving

- The Eight Laws Governing Self-Care

- The Eight Laws Governing Healthy Change

- The Eight Laws Governing A Healthy Workplace

(To license these materials contact: webmaster@compassionfatigue.org)

Coming Soon!

- *30 Days to Healthy Caregiving: A Practical Plan For Managing Compassion Fatigue*

COMPASSION FATIGUE
AWARENESS PROJECT°

Printed by the Compassion Fatigue Awareness Project©

Patricia Smith, Founder

Patricia@compassionfatigue.org

www.compassionfatigue.org

For permissions, contact Derek Smith, Webmaster, web@
compassionfatigue.org

Disclaimer

This information is presented for educational purposes only. It is not a substitute for informed medical advice or training. Do not use this information to diagnose or treat a health problem without consulting a qualified health or mental health care provider. If you have concerns, contact your health care provider, mental health professional, or your community health center.

CPSIA information can be obtained at www.ICGtesting.com
Printed in the USA
LVOW06s1612060514

384630LV00002B/574/P